Advance Praise for SKIRTworking[TM]

"The 'good ol' girl network is alive and well! The authors celebrate the fact that women ARE different than men and can build powerful businesses based on those differences. Women are creative, nurturing, and collaborative beings - these innate qualities can and must be leveraged to grow our businesses and to help other women do the same."

– Sandra Sellani,
Author of "What's Your BQ?(Brand Quotient)"
and Brand Consultant

"Women are rock stars in business! For so long, we've heard what we "are not" versus men. Our time has come. Women are being recognized as a force in business. We make businesses stronger and we are starting our own successful businesses in droves.

SKIRT™ and the messages in the book SKIRTworking: How to Network Using SKIRT, helps us recognize how to leverage our strengths as individuals and as a community. In starting my own business, tapping into a community of great women proved to be an invaluable ingredient in my team's successful creation of a strong business that nurtures people and the planet."

– Sheryl O'Loughlin,
CEO/Co-Founder, Nest Naturals
and Former CEO, Clif Bar and Company

"Alberda, Balog and Fleece guide you to think outside the box and find new and innovative ways to build your business without breaking the bank. The ideas taught in this book are a home run!"

– Alexis Martin Neely,
best-selling author of "Wear Clean Underwear!
A Fast, Fun, Friendly - and Essential - Guide
to Legal Planning for Busy Parents"

"This is a great way for all professional women to put their female strengths to work and build a substantial book of business! SKIRTworking will teach you how to use talents and skills you already possess to build your business in the most cost-effective manner. You'll not only enjoy using the SKIRTWorking system, it will give you a financial leg-up on your competition."

"Every woman running a business, or thinking of starting one, should apply these innovative SKIRTworking techniques if they want to be successful."

"Finally – a book that teaches women how to achieve success in business by empowering themselves with their innate female qualities, rather than asking women to conform to a man's world. Bravo!"

"I believe women have demonstrated, and businesses have recognized, that women are good communicators and they know when to compromise and when to stand firm. They know how to connect with each other and how to help each other. SKIRTworking ™ is helping other women to be the best they can be."

"SKIRT™ has given me the opportunity to align myself with some of the most dynamic, powerful, and motivating women in my community. SKIRT™ has helped me grow both personally and professionally, and I feel fortunate to work with such fabulous women!"

SkirtWorking™

How To Network Using SKIRT*

MICHELLE ALBERDA
MICHELLE BALOG
and STACEY FLEECE

*SKIRT: Sharing Knowledge, Information & Resources Together

Published by:
Bush Street Press
237 Kearny Street, #174
San Francisco, CA 94108
www.bushstreetpress.com
email: press@bushstreetpress.com
Phone: 888-451-8917

ISBN-13 978-0-9794245-1-9

Library of Congress Control Number: 2008932218
Printed in the United States of America

September 2008

10 9 8 7 6 5 4 3 2 1

Work that SKIRT!

Michelle Alberda

This book is dedicated to all of the fabulous women in SKIRT™ Network, San Francisco. Thank you for believing in SKIRTworking and for joining us on this incredible journey. It has been amazing to watch all of you grow in your personal and professional lives. You continue to inspire us!

Contents

Introduction ix

How To Use This Book xii

Chapter One: What Is SKIRT™? 1

Chapter Two: Feminine But Fearless 7

Chapter Three: Nurturing And Networking 27

Chapter Four: Ask And You Shall Receive 39

Chapter Five: Keeping It In The Family 57

Chapter Six: Calendered Contacts 67

Chapter Seven: The Ladies Who Lunch 71

Chapter Eight: How To Start Your Own
              SKIRT™ Network 77

Chapter Nine: Implementing SKIRT™ Strategies
              In Your Business 101

Chapter Ten: Tapping Into Your SKIRT™ Power
              To Develop Your Average Power 119

Women refer 236% more prospects than men.

Source: Working Woman magazine
1999 Readers Study

"Since 2005, SKIRT™ Network is the ONLY business marketing I need to do."

Michelle Alberda,
Financial Advisor

"SKIRT™ Network member referrals resulted in over $100K of my annual gross sales. My active involvement in SKIRT™ Network, San Francisco has significantly increased my client base and has helped me rank as a top-10 producer company-wide for the last two years."

Stacey Fleece,
Senior Loan Consultant,
San Francisco Mortgage Broker

Introduction

Congratulations are in order! You are about to discover the secret to networking success, which can help you catapult your business to a whole new level. Take the time to read this book from cover to cover and you'll discover the means to build a powerful business network – the type of network most business professionals only dream about.

By the time you finish this book, you will know how to network effectively. Better still, you will have the knowledge and skills to develop your own SKIRT™ Network, bringing together like-minded professional women with the common goal of building their businesses on referrals. Each one of these women will be an invaluable resource for you.

Not only is this book a practical guide to networking, it is also a comprehensive guide that will teach you a secret truth about women. It is a unique tool that will propel you forward to your SKIRTworking destiny! Get ready to discover our secret and yours: women are natural networkers. By writing this book, we transfer this knowledge to you – that, as women, if we apply our natural skills, we can take the business world by storm.

Think about it, and you won't be surprised. Our position in society as nurturers endows us with the ability to bring people together in a positive and highly productive fashion. Can you think of a better way to broker business deals and develop professional relationships? The concepts of SKIRT™ and SKIRTworking come from this idea that women are natural connectors.

Before we go any further, however, we should take a quick look at the current situation of businesswomen. Where do we stand in the business world?

According to the National Association of Women Business Owners (NAWBO):

- Women-owned businesses now exceed 10 million in the United States.

- From 1997 – 2004, the number of women-owned firms in the US grew at twice the rate of all US firms, and employment grew at two times the national average.

- One in every 11 adult women owns a business.

- Female entrepreneurs generate nearly $2.5 trillion in revenue to the US economy each year.

- Businesses run by women employ more than 19 million people.

- The number of minority women-owned firms increased by 32% between 1997 and 2002 at a rate four times faster than that of all US firms.

- Female business owners will spend an estimated $546 billion annually on salaries and benefits.

- As a percentage of all businesses in the United States, women-owned businesses represent almost 50%.

Bottom line: our influence is substantial, and continues to grow. In what once was a decidedly male-dominated world, the balance is shifting and the future looks very encouraging. Women, both outside and inside the corporate world, are a force to be reckoned with and our collective strength is growing. More important, perhaps, we are also effecting major changes in business.

Carol Kuc, President of the Board of Directors of NAWBO, suggests that networking may be one of the principle reasons why women are becoming so incredibly successful in business. "Women and men business owners have different management styles," she points out. "Women emphasize relationship building as well as fact gathering."

The simple truth about women is that we build relationships by nurturing and attending to the needs and interests of others. SKIRT™, an acronym that stands for Sharing Knowledge Information & Resources Together, is a concept established in full recognition of the way women naturally network. Applying these principles, we have created the concept of SKIRTworking.

How To Use This Book

Though this book was written with a focus on female entrepreneurs, it will also be helpful for women holding or looking to hold management positions at small companies or large corporations. The advice in these pages will be useful to any woman in business for whom success is largely dependent upon building a strong network. Upon finishing the book, go back and peruse the easy-to-use checklists to accomplish the simple steps. For additional tools, refer to our website: www.skirtworking.com.

This book will teach you the following:

- How to generate unlimited referrals.
- Why the SKIRT™ networking strategy is so effective.
- The amazing innate powers that make women better net-workers than men.
- Why nurturing is an important part of successful SKIRTworking.
- How to nurture your professional ambitions with the support of like-minded professional women.
- Why personal growth is important to your professional life.
- What it takes to transform you from an average networker into a superpower SKIRTworker!
- How to implement SKIRT™ strategies in your business.
- How to set up your own SKIRT™ Network.

So, find yourself a quiet place, pour yourself a cup of tea, open your mind and get ready to rock your world!

skirt [skurt] (n.d.). Dictionary.com Unabridged (v 1.0.1).

- *noun,* The part of a gown, dress, slip, or coat that extends downward from the waist. 2. The boarding marginal or outlying part of a place, group, etc. 3. *slang,* A woman or girl. 4. *verb,* To avoid, keep distance from. 5. *acronym,* SKIRT™ A group of women brought together to generate referrals, improve their businesses, and help others by Sharing Knowledge Information & Resources Together!

Chapter One:
What Is SKIRT™?

Before we discuss the specifics of our SKIRTworking methods, it's important to establish how the SKIRT™ Network began in June 2005.

As professionals, we have known each other for years, and have frequently worked together on deals as well as philanthropic causes. Ultimately, SKIRT™ was born out of our deep mutual respect for each other's professional aptitudes and abilities. It's also important to note that our respective businesses provide services that are somewhat related (Real Estate Brokerage, Mortgage Brokerage and Financial Planning). Over the years, we have found many opportunities to refer our clients back and forth to each other. These referrals helped each of our individual businesses prosper to the point that we saw the innate value of personal and business relationships. Because of this bond, we named ourselves the "dream team."

During a luncheon celebrating the close of a deal all three of us had worked on, we had a revelation: We realized we enjoyed such great success when referring clients to each other, why not expand our circle of influence to provide the same sort of network pool for other professionals and their clients? Why not enable and encourage other professional women to refer their clients to us and to each other, and set about establishing a group of trusted and well-respected "get-it-done" professionals? We quickly realized we would not only learn from each other, but help each other grow our businesses through referrals. What resulted from this thinking was SKIRT™ – a business networking group of female entrepreneurs. In time, we would not only share our marketing and business development secrets, but we would enjoy the trust and respect that comes from belonging to a cohesive team.

We made lists of people to invite to the inaugural meeting of the SKIRT™ Network. The members, by and large, would either be self-employed or working at a company that expected them to generate their own business leads. When considering the likely member profile of the SKIRT™ Network, it was obvious it would be a group for women. The more we thought about it, the more it made sense: women, after all, make much better networkers.

SKIRT's goal, as a cohesive group of professionals, was to Share Knowledge Information & Resources Together. We also wanted to communicate our desire to effect change in the business world. The name SKIRT™ also established our desire to support and strengthen the position of women. Although we respect the position of men, and certainly don't consider male business contacts irrelevant, we want SKIRT™ to be a celebration of the power of women in business.

Our first SKIRT™ meeting consisted of seven people. Today, the group's membership is dynamic (it has been as large as 27) and we now have an extensive waiting list of women who want to join. Most importantly, however, we've grown together as a resource team, a mentoring and nurturing team, and a support team for all involved. Every member takes away something personal from our meetings. Our SKIRT™ Network has not only enhanced our lives financially, but also empowered us emotionally and spiritually.

After a successful three years, it's our goal to share what we've learned and support other professional women in developing their own SKIRT™ Network.

As you read this book, we'll assume you have a unique product or service to offer. If you work for a company, we'll assume your job or corporate success depends upon your networking ability. We'll also assume that, thus far, you've had commendable success in developing your business or market penetration. You know, however, that your full potential has yet to be realized.

You could spend tons of money on advertising in print publications or trade magazines. You could exhibit at industry-related conferences and trade shows. You could spend hours, days, and weeks chasing down leads and get nowhere. Or, you could tap into your feminine power and nurture the business relationships you already have, creating marketing success and boosting your sales for pennies on the dollar.

With an arsenal of professional-minded women, ready and available to support you, time will make you your clients' and colleagues' ultimate "cog in the wheel." Trust us, that is what you want to be. Tucked carefully into position, you'll find your clients, friends and colleagues reaching out to you for reliable referrals and meaningful recommendations. Within your own SKIRT™ Network, you'll be able to interact with service providers and vendors you trust to service your clients as well as you do. It's a good feeling to be a continuous resource for your client, even long after your initial business is done.

Case in point, the Financial Planner had tried every traditional type of networking and client acquisition technique to build a successful system for generating referrals. With each, she enjoyed some success, but after evaluating each opportunity in depth, she realized the return on investment for time and energy was actually pretty low. She determined that her participation in SKIRT™ Network was by far the most efficient and cost-effective way of promoting herself and her business. Her results have been duplicated by countless other SKIRT™ members.

Here's a rundown on the main reasons why SKIRT™ is so successful for generating referrals:

Time: SKIRT™ Network requires a two hour commitment from members and a four hour commitment from the leadership board each month.
Total Time Commitment: Two - Four hours per month.

Cost: SKIRT™ meetings are free for members. (Of course, we take turns bringing refreshments and hosting the meetings, but the cost works out to approximately $100 a year for food and beverages. In other words, for $100 a year, the Financial Planner receives 75% of her referrals.) It has got to be the most cost-effective means of generating referrals and acquiring clients...EVER!
Total Cost: (Practically) Zero

Effort: How much effort do we have to expend to make our SKIRT™ Network effective? Monthly meetings are fun, and members love telling others about the women in our SKIRT™ Network. Generating referrals for others is effortless! And while referring potential clients to our fellow members, we know potential clients are being referred to us as well.
Total Effort: Zero

Already you should see the emerging pattern – a high return for smart networking. Before we reveal more secrets to SKIRTworking success, it's important to first address the underlying reasons why women avoid using their natural networking skills.

CHAPTER TWO:

Feminine But Fearless

L et's face it: Women should naturally be better at networking than men. The key word here is "naturally". Dr. Douglas B. Richardson, in an article found on CareerJournal.com, interviewed women regarding their opinions about men in business. One of the most common complaints was that men are generally terrible networkers; they are not naturally nurturing or supportive. Most of the women interviewed said that men were often "frustrating, demeaning and unproductive" in the business environment. The broader inference is that most men in business aren't willing to help secure the interests of others. They compartmentalize, dividing business from the personal, and vice versa. They don't see it as their responsibility to embody any of the positive relationship qualities in their business dealings that they may very well apply in their personal relationships. The women interviewed for this article jokingly chalked up the extreme cases of this problem to "Male Testosterone Syndrome," or MTS. According to these women, there are five main symptoms of the condition:

1. **Access problems** – As networking contacts, some men are difficult to reach, particularly for women, and are reluctant to return phone calls related to networking opportunities. In person, some men act cliquish, clannish, and clubby around female professionals, which is behavior hardly conducive to business collaboration.

2. **Condescension** – Men suffering from severe forms of MTS think they know everything and, therefore, there is no reason to listen to another's point of view. In milder cases, this symptom presents as a simple inability to adapt in response to new ideas or suggestions.

3. **Dominance** – In the overwhelming majority of instances, men don't collaborate well in business because they are threatened easily and prefer to dominate. For men with extreme cases of MTS, every conversation might as well be a competition.

4. **Tactlessness** – What men like to call "brutal honesty" is often rude, coarse, or boorish.

5. **Callousness** – In extreme cases, men are insensitive, inflexible, and unconcerned with the difference between sympathy and empathy. They are attuned to neither. Many men in business are simply not attuned to other people's feelings or don't realize the need to be.

Of course, none of these symptoms are applicable to all men, but you get the general idea. Women, by and large, are more willing to collaborate and to assist each other in building business networks. They rarely take competition to extremes. They are generally more receptive to new ideas and more willing to help than our male counterparts. It's a difference in approach that stems in part from nature and from our experiences under that perennial "glass ceiling" of the corporate world. Even today, women still hold a minority of management positions in business, and are under-represented on boards in the non-profit sector. While the difference in pay between men and women has decreased over the past decade, a disparity still exists there too. If women want to succeed in a professional world that is still largely male-dominated, who better to depend on than each other for a hand up?

Let's also consider the possibility that there are fundamental personality differences between the sexes, and these differences make women better networkers. This is the idea that we've been leading up to, but we're certainly not the first to realize it. The Myers-Briggs Type Indicator, a well-known tool for measuring individual styles and preferences, differentiates between "thinking" and "feeling" styles of decision-making. "Thinkers" believe decisions should be rational and logical, and that the world is colored in black and white. They also tend to believe there are consistent rules that have very little, if any, flexibility and that emotions can weaken the overall effectiveness of the decision-making process. "Feelers", on the other hand, value emotion in the decision-making process and in any actions that come as a result of their decisions. For a "feeler", there are no absolute rights and wrongs, no hard rules; the best decision is the one that helps everyone walk away from the table feeling as good as possible.

It is not surprising that approximately two-thirds of all men who take the Myers-Briggs test are categorized as "thinkers," while about two-thirds of the women are categorized as "feelers" based on their scores. The Myers-Briggs test reinforces the case that women make better networkers, because to network effectively, you must be collaborative, adapting, able to facilitate consensus and, above all, nurturing. Women, as "feelers", maintain these characteristics in both their personal and professional lives. As "thinkers", men have a hard time collaborating precisely because the process requires flexibility and typically does not allow you to follow a set of rules or protocols. In essence, it's the difference between a round table and a rectangular table. At a round table, everyone is equal. With a rectangular table, someone has to be at the head and everyone else has a definite place. How can men be effective networkers if they are fundamentally built as "thinkers" and have no experience operating as "feelers"?

One problem, however, is that the "thinker" style dominates the business world. Though women have the inherent qualities that should make them good networkers, these same qualities hold them back in the "thinker" dominated environment. Women are frequently afraid of the following:

- Asking for money.
- Asking for help.
- Being too pushy.
- Inconveniencing others.
- Putting our needs before others.
- Seeming 'sales-y'.

This is our own internal negative self-talk and it needs to be quashed. Negative self-talk is primarily a manifestation of our doubts and insecurities. As women, we frequently battle with this flawed mindset. The best way to overcome negative self-talk is to focus on personal growth. What is personal growth? Personal growth is the process of knowing thyself, improving thyself, and loving thyself.

Know Thyself

In the sixth century, a Delphic Oracle proclaimed: "Know thyself". Knowing yourself includes indentifying your strengths and weaknesses. How do we recognize our weaknesses, and learn not to hide behind them? How do we discover or confirm our strengths and learn to celebrate them? How do we become balanced?

We achieve balance by being honest with ourselves. Unapologetic, no-nonsense honesty. Indentifying and embracing our weakness can be a truly liberating experience. For instance, your associates know that you are the scattered, creative type that develops fierce million dollar ideas, yet have tepid organization and management skills. So what? Instead of pretending you are something you are not – an organized, multi-tasker - fess up and recognize your weaknesses for what they are: areas that need improvement. You have two choices: either improve upon your weaknesses or acknowledge them, move on and focus on your strengths. The same holds true about your strengths. If you are a solid artist, focus on that. Maybe the money isn't flowing, but as the old saying goes: Energy flows where attention goes. Your strengths will magnify the more you focus on them. It's funny, the more the members of the "dream team" pat ourselves on the back and celebrate our personal and financial successes, the more success we attract. When you are positive and revel in your strengths, only more good can come about. Always remember, the purpose of evaluating your weaknesses is not to make you feel miserable or frustrated. In the same way, recognizing your strengths isn't designed to make you conceited. Both are necessary for developing self-awareness.

Learning to understand your own personality type and the types of others is empowering. You will be able to appreciate why people react differently in different situations. Eventually, you will be better able to accept and understand people's behaviors that differ from your own. These insights will make you much more centered and better able to deal with people, an essential skill for generating contacts. You are going to need people no matter what your area of expertise and no matter what type of business you have. You will come to understand the all too important reality that you cannot be responsible for other people's behavior. The only behavior you can control is your own.

Fear seems to be a deterrent for women in business. We fear inadequacy, ineffectiveness. In some instances we're afraid of success, too. Perhaps we feel it sets the bar higher in other aspects of our lives. To overcome this fear and achieve success interacting with others, we need to realize our potential.

Getting in touch with your true self is part of this realization process. It is also a positive step towards promoting an open yet functioning mind.

Although we don't think about it much, courage is also a vital ingredient for personal growth and business success. Of course, courage is also important in SKIRTworking.

Most people accept courage as a quality reserved for soldiers, firefighters, and activists. Most are happy cowering behind the walls of our own limited perceptions. We're even persuaded not to be too bold or too brave in most situations and contexts, since courage and bravery are advertised as being too dangerous. This outlook doesn't do much for our business interests.

A side effect of overemphasizing the importance of personal security is that many people now live reactively. We're talking in terms of everything from their personal lives to their professional lives. Instead of setting their own goals, making plans to achieve them, and implementing those plans, most people are trying to play it safe to the point of inertia. People don't work to improve their relationships to make them satisfying. Most people simply don't make the effort to improve their lives. The direction life takes is left to chance due to fear or the unwillingness to rock the boat and change course.

To get the most out of SKIRTworking, you must recognize the huge gulf between recklessness and courage. If you haven't taken control of your life and your networking up to this point, ask yourself now what you're afraid of:

- Success
- Failure
- Rejection
- Poverty
- Humiliation
- Speaking Publicly
- Regret

It's time to recognize your fears and put them behind you. Once you've identified them, you can isolate and eradicate them. Don't let yourself become preoccupied with the idea of security, with what's familiar. Be courageous: you have your intelligence and common sense to identify and navigate any real dangers. An important aspect of personal growth involves seeing things for what they are and building the confidence to trust your instincts and other innate senses. You are the best judge of what is actually dangerous so long as you consciously work to be self-aware.

SKIRTworking should lead you to be bold when it comes to promoting your business. Reach out to other professionals and be bold about asking for what you want. Try asking yourself how you would behave if you no longer felt fear as an emotion. Common responses suggest people would speak up more often, talk to more strangers, ask for more sales, and take on more ambitious projects. What if you managed to do something you're afraid of? What if you enjoyed it? The achievement could make all the difference in your life by boosting your confidence. The worst-case scenario: you have to try harder to overcome your fear the next time.

An important step on the path to becoming a bold human being and a top SKIRTworker: accept that there is really no good or logical reason why you shouldn't do what you want, so long as you don't hurt other people or yourself. It isn't rude to introduce yourself to a stranger. You shouldn't avoid public speaking because you think you don't have anything to say. You have something worthwhile to share with people. You have a range of experiences to talk about. Are you a parent? Are you a spouse? Are you in business for yourself? In becoming a SKIRTworker you have dreams and aspirations you're trying to achieve. These are all experiences that people want to hear about, that give you something to contribute.

Think about how your life would change if you could confidently and courageously do these things without fear. You don't have to stand up and give a one-hour talk on a topic of your choice. You don't ever have to make a public speech of any kind. The point is more that you shouldn't be afraid and shun the opportunity if it happens to come your way.

Personal growth can also include the process of overcoming fear on many levels. The word courage derives from the Latin cor, meaning "heart", but think of it this way: courage is not only about heart, but about what you feel and invest in a situation emotionally. Courage has a lot to do with how you think, with the brain and specifically the neo-cortex. This is one of the most distinctly human parts of us. To be courageous and face your fears, you actually have to battle with the "fight or flight" mechanism instilled by none other than your brain. To actually conquer a fear response – let's say a fear response to speaking in front of a room full of people – we actually have to shift control away from the emotional limbic brain we share in common with other mammals, and apply the reasoning powers of the neo-cortex to assess whether the danger is real. You will feel when the fear isn't real. In other words, you'll rationalize whether you need to be running or not. If you know a fear is irrational and you take action anyway, the term "Are you man or mouse?" becomes a valid question. The more you learn to act despite being afraid, the more evolved your approach. Becoming an evolved human being is the ultimate goal of personal growth, no matter what particular path you are on. As for SKIRTworking, well, if you want to get the most out of this approach to promoting your business and yourself, it definitely helps to be able to ask for what you want upfront, talk comfortably to a large group of people, and seek out whatever you need to promote your business unabashed.

Being courageous doesn't mean you go looking for trouble. It doesn't even mean that you go looking for the opportunities to do something you have been afraid of; it's primarily about being brave when you have to be and making the most of opportunities that do come your way. You can't dictate what opportunities you have and how those opportunities are manifested. You never know exactly what the next step is going to be and if you try to predict it, you essentially limit yourself to a number of outcomes. If you allow yourself to be afraid of anything to the point that you avoid it, then you've limited the opportunities you have to achieve your goal; in this case, you've limited the opportunities you have to become successful – no matter what that means to you. Is your fear really worth that much?

Courage in the context of personal growth is something that many philosophers and thinkers have written about. Ambrose Redmoon, for example, wrote that "Courage is not the absence of fear, but rather the judgment that something else is more important than fear." Mark Twain wrote that "Courage is resistance to fear, mastery of fear - not absence of fear." John Wayne said that "Courage is being scared to death, but saddling up anyway."

Anais Nin, the French writer, neatly summarized the effect that courage and fear have on your life in regards to opportunities and possibilities. She said "Life shrinks or expands in proportion to one's courage". In other words, the more courageous you are, the more your life and the opportunities in it will expand. As you let fear take control, your opportunities are greatly reduced. In the words of Eleanor Roosevelt: "You gain strength, courage, and confidence by every experience in which you really stop to look fear in the face. You are able to say to yourself, 'I have lived through this horror. I can take the next thing that comes along.' You must do the thing you think you cannot do."

The more readily you are able to address your fears and overcome them, the faster you'll develop new skills and the ability to be a success by your own definition, emotionally and financially. You will develop the ability to transform your business, if this is a goal you have in mind, finding referrals for more clients just by showing up and being present at a SKIRT™ meeting.

By living consciously and investing in every decision you make, you put yourself in the position to achieve. You have a choice: either exercise your human courage and consciousness or admit that your fears are too much for you, and embrace life as a mouse. SKIRTwork, try something innovative, or stick with the old and ineffective networking. You get the idea, right? You've got to make this choice consciously and with full awareness of its consequences.

If you decide to be courageous and embark on a path of personal development in every area of your life (and this is the best way to make the most of the potential of SKIRTworking), you will be well on your way to living consciously and achieving your goals. You should also bear in mind that along the way you may have some dysfunctional relationships, you may be broke at one time, and you may even fail completely at some point. It's impossible to predict exactly what will happen even if we plan and work hard. In the long run, persistence pays off. Don't be put off when you can't micromanage your life. SKIRTworking proves that the most effective way to network is to go natural, to seek out natural connections with like-minded women, other professionals. Why should any other aspect of life be different? Even the worst, most devastating failures are all just milestones along the path of a life lived courageously. You'll always have your private victory as a conscious person, with the very best abundance of joy, happiness, and fulfillment in your life.

If you give in to your fears, you only make them stronger and yourself less so. Similarly, when you avoid your fears and feel relieved that you escaped feeling embarrassed or afraid, you implement a psychological reward that reinforces the avoidance behavior. You are all the more likely to avoid what you fear in the future and you condition yourself to become timid and to avoid challenges that might lead to success. Unless you nip this behavior in the bud, you sabotage your own success. Courageous people are still afraid, but they work to prevent their fears from paralyzing them.

Instead of letting yourself become stuck in a rut, get in touch with your own intuition. Listen to the voice in the back of your head telling you every day that you have the ability to run a thriving business and develop an effortless network by SKIRTworking with other brilliant and talented women who can bring you great clients – people you are actually excited to work with. It's like the voice you heard when you were a child, on those days when it seemed the whole world was waiting for you, your whole life in front of you. Most people, as they grow older, settle into their fears and the pattern of their life that doesn't require any effort. They switch off or generally drown out the little voice. If you think about it, as we said earlier, it's the little voice that is telling you to reach out to new people and like-minded professionals in the first place.

You ignore the voice that wants you to succeed; perhaps you drown it out by watching television or working long hours, by drinking alcohol or caffeine. Some drown it out by overeating or under-eating. Whatever your drug of choice happens to be, it's important to identify it, and, if you're serious about achieving any of your goals, put a stop to the negative behaviors right away. If you ignore the encouraging voice, you do so at your detriment and at your own risk!

Whenever you drown out that little voice telling you to do better, you're lowering your level of consciousness. You're moving closer to becoming an instinctive animal and further away from becoming a conscious human being. You react to life instead of proactively going after your goals and fall into a state of learned helplessness.

Putting an end to the vicious cycle is to summon your courage and confront that inner voice. Sit down with a pen and a piece of paper. Using a computer is okay too, but handwriting is better for a spiritual release of your feelings. Think about what the little voice in your head is saying. Write down everything and then think about what it all means for you.

Ask yourself these questions and write down your responses:

- What do I want to achieve for myself in business?
- What do I need to change about myself to achieve my goals?
- How am I going to use networking to achieve my goals?
- Why have I waited until now to begin this process?

These are just some of the questions you should be asking yourself to get a clear idea of where you are at the moment as a business professional, as a networker, and as an individual. Remember that no part of you exists in isolation from the rest. To be effective in life, you have to be balanced, centered, and respectful of all the roles you play.

In order to know yourself, you should also evaluate your UQ (Utility Quotient). Other names for this include "emotional competence" or "emotional intelligence". Some of your intelligence is inherited while some of it is developed based on your environment growing up. Your utility quotient score is based on how well you actually use your talents. You get a high score when you make an effort to achieve, when you actively look to build your knowledge base and make use of the skills and resources you already have. This is to be differentiated from your IQ (or Intelligence Quotient) which basically measures how smart you are measured by your performance on various standardized tests. Most IQ tests include exercises from a variety of domains. There are generally items that gauge short-term memory, verbal knowledge, spatial visualization, and perceptual speed. Unfortunately, there is no way of knowing exactly how accurate a measurement an IQ score is of your intelligence. Not to mention the fact that smart people don't always live up to their potential and some people who are not as smart actually make millions, sometimes billions of dollars in business and prove to be terrific networkers.

The point is, even if you have an average IQ, if you develop an above average UQ, you're probably going to do as well or better than people who have a higher IQ. Take one example from a business executive. He's fifty-something now with a wife and kids; he has an English literature degree from Oxford and an MBA from Harvard. He's currently unemployed. A brilliant man intellectually speaking, but for all his brilliance he can neither hold a high paying job long-term nor do enough to apply himself to start his own business. In fact, this individual never managed to tap into what was potentially an invaluable and inexhaustible network of contacts from his days at university and in business. He was only prepared to reach out to contacts when the need was immediate and pressing. He had no foresight or interest in building relationships and networks of contacts to apply.

Increasing your utility quotient means identifying and making the most of your personal strength, looking to increase it, build upon it, and focus it to use it to your best advantage. How often have you had a great idea to do something with your business? Probably you've had more than one. You may have realized how good the idea was as well. You might even have thought about implementing it. Still, if you're reading this book, you probably haven't managed to follow through. Not yet, anyway. You probably drew a blank on whom to go to for advice or else you were simply too uncomfortable to ask for help.

Most people have a problem with follow-through. Networking effectively takes a lot of strength. It takes strength, confidence, agility, intelligence, and fearlessness!

Improve Thyself

To build your personal strength you need to know who you are, be in touch with what you want, understand your strengths and weaknesses, and know that how you use your given talents is the best indicator of how successful you can be (IQ versus UQ).

Ask yourself how often you have tried something and simply given up because you couldn't find the time to follow through.

How often have you simply filed away an idea or run into a roadblock and not asked for help?

By working to increase your personal strength, you'll develop the ability to stick with the work, to keep going when things seem difficult and ask for help when needed. You become more awake, more aware. To grow spiritually is actually to become more aware of who you really are and be in a much better position to get what you want.

How does one increase their personal strength?

- Write down three to five things you did well each day before you go to bed.
- List three things you can do in a day to build your confidence. Then, work to make these things daily habits and incorporate them into your lifestyle.
- Learn something new as this will increase your overall confidence level.
- Remember that confidence comes from taking risks. Don't be afraid to take risks, even when you don't yet feel confident in yourself. Confidence will come slowly.
- Appreciate who you are and what you already have.
- Repeat affirmations every day, when you wake up and before you go to sleep.
- Ask questions when you don't know the answers.

The best way to develop your potential is to identify your talents. Looking at your potential will help you add skills and knowledge to your repertoire. This will help you develop a consistent, near-perfect performance in whatever you want to do; it will hone your networking skills until there's very little effort required for you to secure what you want and need from other people.

Research shows that people learn, change, and improve the most in those areas of the brain that already have the strongest synaptic connections. As Joseph LeDoux, professor of neuroscience at NYU, said in *The Four Disciplines of Sustainable Growth:* "New [synaptic] connections formed by activity are not created as entirely new entities, but rather are added to . . . pre-existing connections. Added connections are therefore more like new buds on a branch rather than new branches. Activity thus does not produce wholesale rewiring of the brain."

This means that you learn new things and achieve more by working from your strengths. Focusing on your strengths to develop your confidence and personal endurance will increase your performance. The better you are able to stick with the task at hand, the more likely you are to succeed in creating wealth. Effort is required and increased personal strength will help you sustain the necessary effort.

Love Thyself

To attract good things into your life and to start creating a profitable network of contacts, you need to first love and accept yourself. Change occurs most readily and most effectively when you have a personal foundation of self-acceptance and self-love. Nurturing yourself is essential to building a successful career or business and creating success all around. When you love yourself, you can create a life you love and make use of whatever resources are available to you.

Unfortunately, society doesn't support this notion. It doesn't recognize that self-love is necessary for personal happiness and success. Most people, when they receive a compliment, say something to undercut the achievement. They say "it's nothing" or they try and deflect the praise by changing the subject. When networking, it's unlikely that these same people are going to effectively build a network of people they can go to for referrals or any others sort of help.

The interesting thing is that when you brush off a compliment, you're not really doing anyone a favor, least of all yourself. Start to consider compliments as gifts. You wouldn't toss a gift aside. You would accept it and be grateful. You'd say "thank you" and be glad for what you'd received. Start responding in the same way to compliments and you will be well on your way to recognizing your strengths in a way that will have a positive impact on your life.

Understanding and appreciating your own talents will help you to become more confident and centered in your life. Successful business people understand the importance of being this way. It's part of the process for becoming wealthy. Financial stability and richness follow in the footsteps of personal stability and confidence. If you're networking to expand your business and create wealth, you definitely need to bear this in mind.

Put your life in perspective. Everything you've done, everyone you've loved, every mistake you've made, and every obstacle you've overcome is part of the person you are today, and has a bearing on how you engage with others and how you do business.

When you are comfortable that you know enough about yourself, your strengths and weaknesses, and you've embarked officially on the road to self-improvement, it is time to determine where you want to go in life. If you're reading this book, you need to develop a roadmap to track how you are going to achieve the level of business success you want through networking.

CHAPTER THREE:

Nurturing And Networking

Women of the Future: Alternative Scenarios is an article written by futurist and political scientist Christopher Jones. The article was published in *The Futurist* magazine in 1996 and shortly after its publication, several women wrote to express their concerns that the article presented a very one-sided view of the future of women. Several complaints were featured in the Letters to the Editor section of *The Futurist* magazine. In particular, these letters questioned why a man wrote an article discussing the future of women in business. Responding promptly, the editors of the magazine solicited scenarios of a preferred future "for women, by women" to ascertain precisely what women hoped to achieve in the business world. One of the most interesting and popular scenarios called for was an end to the glass ceiling in business as the writers of this segment of the magazine, all female, expressed a desire to see women become entrepreneurs, hiring and mentoring other women to establish equal representation in business.

The female writers called for recognition and celebration of differences between men and women, particularly in terms of management and business enterprises. They even suggested the need for the decentralization of corporations and governments to allow women the opportunity to blend their business and personal activities, balancing interests and ambitions at work with responsibilities at home.

But the role of gender in the work place has been under considerable scrutiny for many decades, at least since the early 1970s. While sex has served as a biological classification, gender, representative of a cultured knowledge, is the classification method that distinguishes women from men. Gender helps us understand cultural dimensions as feminine and masculine, consisting of the values and ideals that originate from culture. In Western societies also, the concept of gender helps to connect the changing conditions for contemporary organizations in addition to the desire, power, and the politics of knowledge.

What we mean by this is actually quite straightforward. What we consider to be masculine and what we consider to be feminine in terms of thoughts, ideas, behaviors, and appearances (physical characteristics) are attributed to the idea of gender, their classification justified as the application of gender difference.

In the work environment, the perceptions of differences between masculine and feminine are particularly problematic. You probably know this already. What we call gender conditioning is actually quite a problem within corporations, as institutional contexts impact gender in organizational realities. In the traditional corporate environment, women are naturally pushed into a particular context, molded into a particular role, and regarded in a particular light.

In the corporate environment, following our train of thought from above, we can determine that many men still maintain a certain limited, highly subjective view of women. The view applies in the business world as much as any other. While once upon a time women worked mostly as secretaries, nurses, or teachers, men seemed to have formed an opinion that it is these roles – characterized as decidedly feminine – that women do best or are otherwise confined to.

Okay, let's face it: men are at least on the right track. If you think about it, secretaries, nurses, and teachers – male or female – tend to be friendly, nurturing, receptive, creative, dependable, and dedicated. They also take on a *feeling* approach to their work. They learn to know and respond to the individual. A secretary will get to know the idiosyncrasies of her boss, not to mention how to organize and connect information so her boss can make use of it. A nurse will anticipate and respond to the needs of her patient. A teacher will get to know a student, applying information to determine the student's strengths, weaknesses, interests, and aspirations.

Let's assume now that these characteristics are part and parcel of every woman's identity. How a person identifies himself or herself and how he or she identifies with others are concepts with enormous consequences for relationships. The ability to see what other people want and need is the first step to building an effective network of contacts. Putting a positive slant on gender differences, Adrienne Snow pointed out: "Gender differences become opportunities for learning and expansion, and they are celebrated."

Recognizing that women are often better networkers than men, let's consider now what exactly networking is (and what it isn't).

First of all, networking is about creating a *network*. If you take a minute, you can probably think of several different types of actual physical networks (e.g., computer networks, company networks, industry networks). Many of these resemble the conceptual network people look for in business. These days, we work with computer networks all the time. Two or more computers can be connected to each other by wires and cables. You can share files, applications. It's possible to share printers and other hardware. You get the idea.

Another example of a network would be, let's say, your local public transportation system. Take the New York Subway system: you have millions of people, residents and tourists, needing to get from A to B. The individual subway lines link together at various key points, such as 42nd Street and 14th Street. You can get from one end of Manhattan to the other, not to mention from the Bronx to Brooklyn or Queens based on the way the various lines link together. Bringing in the buses and even the trains that run as part of the same public transportation system, you find you can get just about anywhere within the five boroughs of New York City.

The idea behind networking is to envision your friends and associates linked together like a physical network. To understand what it is to network, imagine yourself doing a dot-to-dot, linking people who could be useful to each other and useful to you.

Networking involves:

- Staying in touch with people you like and respect.
- Introducing yourself to people you don't know.
- Learning to ask key questions about people you meet to gauge what it is they do and aspire to.
- Listening to people.
- Presenting your own interests and goals as effectively as possible based on a given situation.
- Maintaining detailed contact records – not to mention up-to-date marketing materials such as brochures and business plans – to provide basic information about yourself and your business.
- Getting comfortable handing out your card and brochure.
- Improving your public speaking, body language, and social etiquette.
- Brainstorming and following up with people you meet.

Most people don't follow the prescribed steps for networking. Here's an example of typical networking: John checks in with his university friends every few months and, when he finds himself out of a job, is actively taking note of what his friends are doing. He gets in touch with Michael, who he's known for eight years or so. John asks about a job opening and hopes for the best.

This is the way that most people network. They recognize networking as a powerful tool but they don't look to use it on a regular basis unless they need something specific or unless they have a problem. For example, Claire is a physical therapist working in the private health care system. Her friend Lisa is worried about her mother's much needed hip replacement. Lisa contacts Claire and asks her for help getting her mother seen by a top surgeon. One of the best orthopedic surgeons works at Claire's hospital so Lisa knows she can solve a problem with Claire's help.

Without question, SKIRTworking through personal contact is one of the best and easiest ways to form long-term and profitable business relationships. SKIRTworking, as opposed to traditional networking, gives you the power of one-to-one relationship building, which is virtually unrivaled as a marketing and advertising technique, largely because it allows you to work with women who have the same interests and goals as you, at least in terms of their business. SKIRTworking provides the perfect opportunity to help women feel empowered and blessed.

Power is an interesting word as it pertains to networking – and indeed in SKIRTworking – and it's an idea that we'll come back to in a minute. What you really need to focus on at the moment is realizing that the vast majority of top business people and sales professionals in the world today got to where they are now by understanding the advantages of networking and by making an effort to include networking activities on their weekly or even daily to-do list. But it's not just networking that makes these individuals successful. They go beyond networking as it is traditionally defined and conceived by the know-it-alls of business (the ones who are teaching as opposed to doing). Top networkers – men and women – genuinely care about their contacts and actively stay in touch.

The very best business people create networking plans that help them keep in mind whom is likely to have the biggest and most positive impact upon their business, not to mention how to identify individuals they need to seek out in response to a given opportunity.

Using networking in these two contexts – for business or personal reasons – is perfectly fine and valid. But if you're in business, why not use networking on a consistent basis as a positive, proactive tool rather than a reactive, seemingly negative tool?

Business people should be looking for fresh and innovative ideas. They should be working to generate marketing campaigns for products and services that increase profit and effectively increase their market reach. Doing this is not only decidedly easy, it can also be a lot of fun and one of the most relaxing aspects of doing business. Instead of tapping networks when you have a specific problem to deal with, why not look to generate ideas by brainstorming with your friends and associates, the people you would go to if you had a business problem to resolve?

Basically, there are many ways to network with business associates, friends, and relatives who can be of use to you in business. SKIRTworking is such a phenomenal concept because it draws on all of the best techniques.

To network and nurture among professionals effectively –

network to improve your own business prospects or take the initiative to expand your network by giving an associate a boost in the right direction – you need to become the power source for the people you know. Think of Christmas tree lights. The lights are all linked up but you need the power supply to have them all lit up at once.

Power and identity are two key aspects of effective SKIRTworking. They are also important to organizations in various business contexts. In fact, both have become increasingly visible and complicated in many companies as the result of an increase in the number of diversity programs. Many researchers have explored the role of gender in business communication, for example, as a means of defining identity and understanding power. They found a range of information and expression of gender-based differences showing how, in general, men and women interact differently, displaying different leadership and interpersonal communication styles overall.

Men are traditionally more likely to be selected as group leaders than women in business. They also participate more in group discussions in mixed groups but less than women in single-sex groups. Traditional perceptions also establish men as the hunters, and therefore, the presumed leaders.

As nurturers, the traditional image of women puts us in the background. We are seen as focused on dealing with the everyday tasks, the needs-driven minutia. According to yet more gender-based research, women also tend to feel comfortable working for a man, while men feel less comfortable working for a woman.

Many researchers believe women have a greater need for affiliation and a lesser need for achievement. Those women who focus on achievement rather than fitting in are considered anxious, unfeminine, and selfish. They may experience subtle discrimination and role conflict in the business world.

In terms of communication styles, men are more likely to be aggressive or oppositional; they may tease or even berate the people they are talking to. Women are more likely to share stories of experiences and to share ideas in a friendly and supportive way. At least one research study found that even when women adopt male communication styles, they are less likely to be afforded appropriate attention.

If you want to get ahead in business as a woman, if you want to move your career forward or transfer to a new one, you need to develop your SKIRTworking and nurturing skills by getting in touch with your identity and ability to wield power. At the end of the day – and it's particularly true for women – even if you have talent, a great attitude, business savvy, and clearly defined goals, getting through the door often has a lot to do with who you know and the way in which you take charge and seek to promote your own interests.

To wield power effectively, you need to know that there are several different types of power to make use of. There's organizational, interpersonal, and individual power.

Organizational power is based on a person's position within a particular organization, such as a business. Obviously, if you own your own business, you are the most powerful person in that organization. You should, in theory at least, have maximum power and control.

Interpersonal power has to do with relationships. As a mother or wife, for example, you have power of a particular kind over your children and your husband (although they may have power over you, too!).

Finally, individual power reflects your own strengths and abilities and the extent to which you are able to apply them to achieve your goals.

Think for a moment about who you consider to be a particularly powerful person. Power can be measured objectively or subjectively based on an individual's criteria. The structural power of occupations, for example, can be measured objectively. Your power can be measured based on your position within an organization (whether you're the boss, the manager, a sales person, etc.) and also based on things like coded job descriptions (you could be the first or the second assistant, for example). Subjectively measuring power within an organization you might look to assess the values of the individual worker, their perceptions, and experience of power at work.

As an attribute of certain social roles, power helps to position individuals in organizational roles. It also legitimizes actual power behavior, actions that affect the behavior and emotions of other people. If you're running your own business, your use of power is most definitely legitimized behavior. Developed as part of your identity, wielding power is not only necessary, it's highly appropriate.

The relationship between power, networking, nurturing, and identity is based on the following: you need to be comfortable with who you are in order to be powerful, to make decisions for yourself, your family, and your business. You need to be comfortable wielding power in order to make the most of networking as a business practice. Network building is a lot easier if you are able to nurture other business people with similar interests and ambitions to you who may have farther to go in terms of their development in the business world.

Research says that women have the natural ability to be top-notch networkers, as we mentioned at the beginning of this book (it's no less true now, by the way). However, the same research tends to suggest that many women are also uncomfortable when it comes to exercising power. We can also fall victim, one way or another, to the outdated views about the types of jobs that we can and should be doing (incredible as it may seem that such views still carry any weight!).

CHAPTER FOUR:

Ask And You Shall Receive

N ow it's time to set the record straight about how to get things done, whether it's SKIRTworking for your business or anything else. All those people who told you to wait for perfection – you know who they are…people who tell you to wait for the right job, the right time, the right man – block them out. On close inspection, you'll realize that these people don't really have anything figured out in their own lives. They are using you as a means to overcome their own unhappiness and failings. In short – and not to put too fine a point on it – they don't know what they're talking about.

Sure, what we just said seems to undermine this entire enterprise. Well, not quite. We're not going to try to convince you that there's one right choice or one appropriate path. We are, however, going to try to show you that it's up to you to navigate your own life by looking for opportunities to network, riding out the waves of life as effectively as possible.

Rather than slowing down or even stopping altogether, we suggest a more proactive approach. You need to realize that you only have one shot at this life (at least according to most of the major religions). If we assume that there is only one life apportioned to each of us, what do you think makes more sense? Delaying the pursuit of your dreams until you've achieved absolute control over your life...or taking life as it comes at you, pursuing your dreams and adapting and changing to meet the demands of the situations in which you find yourself? What makes more sense? Waiting for the opportunity to make use of your contacts or seizing the opportunity to put your contacts to work?

Here's some food for thought. In her article, "Women, Repeat This: Don't Ask, Don't Get", Linda Babcock talks about her experiences of the haves and have-nots. While an associate professor, she explains, she watched two of her male colleagues – equal to her in terms of education and experience – each receive promotions. Oh, goodie, she thought, I'm going to get promoted too. Time goes by, however, and no promotion, *What's the deal?*

Sexism and shortsightedness on the part of her boss? Not at all. The two men went ahead and asked for promotions. They were qualified so they got them. For a time, Linda sat around waiting for her boss to realize that she too was qualified and deserving of a promotion. She internalized her frustration. When she plucked up the courage to ask for a promotion herself, she got exactly what she wanted.

Women seem to have trouble asking for what they want. It doesn't matter whether it is business-related or something to do with relationships, family, friends, or significant others. Either we're afraid to ask or we simply don't believe we deserve to get what we want and we become afraid of being branded as overly ambitious, pushy, and power-hungry.

The problem is – and Linda Babcock outlines it pretty well – if you think it makes sense to stand still until you have total control of your life, well, good for you. It's unlikely you're going to have much success networking or creating a successful business. On the other hand, if you're beginning to see the logic of moving ahead, of thinking on the spot in terms of how to make use of your contacts and promote your business interests, give yourself a definite pat on the back. If you sit around waiting for the right moment to come along, you're going to be waiting around your entire life.

One of the reasons many people (men and women) struggle with networking is that you have to know what you want and be prepared to ask for it. You're the only one who can achieve your goals so you shouldn't spend your time trying to live up to other people's expectations. Instead of waiting around, pick the direction you want to go and start planning your next move.

Life is unpredictable, and the same goes for the business world. You'll always be navigating twist and turns. You'll often be guessing about the best way to go. You never know who is going to be able to help you down the road. Perhaps it will be frustrating; sometimes it might feel like the entire world is out to get you. However, setting your own limits and commanding your own time will give you the advantage of being your own person. And what you do with your life is what's important. If you go after your dreams, even if none of them turn out the way you expected, little else matters. When you're pursuing your dreams, you're going in the right direction and yes, you've got a damn good chance of being happy.

Hesitation leads to devastation. You're going to miss way too many opportunities by allowing yourself to hesitate. Instead of standing there and waiting for everything to be perfect, be like a tennis player...on your toes...going after every chance life throws at you. If you stay on your toes, you can see your way through. Of course, it's often particularly difficult for women to grab life by the horns in this way. For one thing, it's usually women who are expected to be the sensible ones, the voices of reason. We're also racked by guilt when we have to divide up our time between our responsibilities, our work, our partners, and our kids. On the face of it, being the voice of reason, being sensible, responsible, and fair to everyone, seems to fly in the face of taking chances and going with the flow. Perhaps it does. We don't have all the answers, but so long as you take care of yourself and your dependents, well, you're good to go. And whoever said it's always in the best interest of the people who depend on you for you to be restrained?

Think about it, if people never took chances in life, they might never secure a positive future for themselves and their families. The chances of becoming a famous actress, Julia Roberts, for example, are pretty slim. Think it's just a matter of beauty and connections? Nope, wrong again.

Think of people you've seen and read about. Look at the likes of Lucille Ball, Billie Jean King, and Erin Brockovich. All of these women have gambled and come out on top. Imitate the initiative of people you admire. Invariably, people who have gotten somewhere in life have taken a couple of chances along the way. They've taken the opportunities in front of them whether or not the opportunities have fit precisely with a plan or a vision they had about their life. There's nothing wrong with having a general idea of where you want to go, but you shouldn't let your image of what your life should be prevent you from pursuing opportunities that don't quite fit with what you had in mind.

You can't predict the path that will get you where you want to go. You can make an educated guess but don't close yourself off. Don't be afraid to take a chance. Don't get too caught up in the planning process. If you spend all of your time planning you won't implement anything – not one of the plans you come up with. If you want to achieve anything in your life, whether it's a great relationship or a fantastic job, stop waiting until you have figured everything out before you act. Jump in the middle of your life and figure it out along the way.

In some cases, it really pays off to be independent and to enforce self-determination. Rules exist in most instances to protect us. For example, the law is designed, on the one hand, to protect citizens, to protect them from others and to protect other people from them. It's against the law for you to drive drunk because you could cause harm to yourself or others. There is, however, a big difference between the laws that protect us from harm and the unwritten rules established by those around us.

When someone tells us we should or shouldn't do something, they probably have our best interests at heart. Most parents mean well when they advise their children against making certain choices. They also mean well – and society means well – by presenting a rather negative front with regard to things like accepting demanding jobs with bad pay, or waiting to go to college. There is a whole range of unwritten doctrines about the way people should live their lives and, for the most part, it is designed and intended to protect people from others and indeed from themselves. On the other hand, no one but you can determine what makes you happy and the reality of many of the unwritten rules is that they look at only part of the argument and some of the evidence. For example, let's consider the unwritten rule about not taking on a demanding job with poor pay. Men and women who work as teachers, as nurses, and as police officers, take on demanding jobs and generally the pay isn't great. They also face some risks. What makes these jobs worthwhile to the individual is presumably the sense of satisfaction, the sheer love of the work.

Another thing to consider: work, and often many other aspects of life, is frequently difficult. What makes it more than just bearable is the happiness, satisfaction, and sense of purpose they offer to the individual. Being a parent, for example, is a struggle. It doesn't matter whether you're a single mom or someone who's raising their kids with friends and family living across the street. At some point, you're going to be frustrated, exhausted, and even bitter. Kids are demanding; raising them requires sacrifices. You might not get to go to the movies like you used to. You don't get as much sleep as you'd like. You and your partner might not enjoy much time to yourselves; well, that's one way of looking at parenthood. Another way is to conclude that there is hardly anything as rewarding as having kids if you want to have them. When you weigh the consequences of your decisions and you know in your heart or in your head that you're going to be happier one way or the other, accept wholeheartedly that ignoring the rules is worth it when the reward you experience is great happiness and personal satisfaction.

What we're saying, though, is that everyone has different wants and perceived needs. In order to achieve your goals, you need to know what you want and need.

Once you believe you know enough about yourself, your strengths and weaknesses, and you've embarked officially on the road to self-improvement, it is time to determine where you want to go in life. You should now understand the importance of creating your success roadmap to achieve your ultimate business and networking goals.

Your Success Roadmap

Imagine you are about to go on a real trip. You're going on an adventure to climb Mount Everest. You have a general idea of where you want to go. You want to get to the top of the mountain, the highest point in the world. It's a fine plan to start with, but you can't actually embark on such a trip without an actual map of where you are going and a plan of how you're going to get to the summit.

In order to ask for what you want, you need to know what you want. If you haven't already created one, you need a business plan to manage and expand your professional enterprise. It is common sense, after all, that if you want to go somewhere, you have to know (or have a general idea) where you're going! Of course, most people don't have a clue how to begin writing their business plan, often because they haven't really thought enough about their business model and whatever particular goals they have in mind. If you haven't thought about how to turn your current business ideas into a reality, then you probably have to spend some more time at the mental drawing board before you start trying to write up the plan you have in your head. We're assuming, of course, that networking is your primary goal at the moment, but the networking agenda for your business should also be established within the context of your own success roadmap.

Although every plan is different, most business plans are not complete without the following components:

Executive Summary – this section describes the basic idea behind the company. For all intents and purposes, this section is the general introduction to the plan. A lot of companies choose to explain the reasons for starting the company in the first place. They may also provide a brief summary of the history of the particular industry to which the venture under scrutiny will revert.

Objectives – presented as bullet points, the objectives of a company are outlined in a business plan so that it is clear to whoever is reading the plan precisely what the goals of the individual and the team might be.

Market Segment Analysis – this section is basically an in depth review of customers and consumers; those you intend to target with your business.

Product/Service Information – explaining the importance of the product or service you're offering is all-important, this section generally includes a review of the product or service pointing out why yours is different from everything else on the market and why there is a substantial need for the product or service.

Marketing Strategies – this section explains how the business will be marketed to various audiences. Most business plans provide a general outline of marketing strategies followed up in a marketing plan.

Sales Strategies – these are crucial to the success of a business so every business plan includes a section devoted to explaining how sales will be achieved. A number of key questions are generally answered: who will be responsible for sales? How will prospects be converted to sales? How will sales be recorded and increased if necessary?

Personnel Information – Business plans generally include a review of the company structure and planning. An important aspect of this is the company staff. Personnel with positions of authority, whether they are managers or executive assistants can have an important role to play in the development and ultimate success of a company. Career experience, education level, assigned responsibilities, and relevant skill sets are generally outlined in this section. Sometimes resumes for personnel are included with the plan.

Financial Summary and Projections – Although financial projections for start-up businesses are generally based on guesswork, they are an important element of a business plan. It is vital to outline cash-flow expectations – money coming in and money going out. Gradually, financial summaries and projections can be updated as more information is collected and the company begins to generate some income.

There are plenty of good books that outline how to write a business plan. A general web search will also produce a range of relevant results. It's important to put time and effort into your plan to get it as close to perfect as you can. Your plan is a blueprint for your company and will help you expand your business as efficiently and effectively as possible.

Get What You Want Out Of Networking

Most small business owners do not fail because their product or service is not good, but because the owner did not spend enough time generating revenue through sales and marketing strategies. While every component of the business plan is important, without revenue, there is not a business. If networking or generating referrals is part of the sales and marketing strategy, the following three steps are essential to get optimal results:

1. Put a stop to negative thinking and turn your unconscious negativity into positive conscious thought.

2. Figure out your networking goals. What do want to gain from your business? How soon do you want to achieve your networking goals? How soon do you want to benefit from

SKIRTworking contacts? Do you want these contacts to help you with marketing, finance, business planning, or sales? Most people who concentrate on networking own their own businesses, but you can also benefit from networking when working for others. Many physicians, attorneys, and corporate executives often achieve considerable success as networkers, deriving great benefits by tapping into networks. Establish your networking goals by talking specifics. Write down your goals and ideas. Once you've done this, you can move onto step three.

3. Develop a strategy to pursue your networking goals. It should be a broad strategy: you need to get in touch with your strengths and weaknesses and determine what you can do to make the most of networking. Remember what we said about balance?

Of course, your business plan is not the only roadmap/blueprint you need. Your business is a crucial part of your effort to become successful but it is by no means the only element. You need to develop a blueprint for yourself in the context of your business, as a networker. To be happy, centered, committed, and focused is essential to becoming good at anything, and it's particularly important to excelling at something like networking. It is next to impossible to be successful if you don't first feel successful and have confidence in yourself. It's not about accepting what you've already achieved as all you can achieve. Feeling successful is about recognizing the positives in your life. It's about realizing that you have already achieved a great deal. You can achieve more, certainly, but you've already achieved a lot. Outline a plan to recognize your track record. Start on a path of self-discovery. Try to become more self-aware. As you do, you'll learn amazing things about yourself that will reinforce your strengths and help to improve your weaker areas.

An important roadmap/blueprint to establish in addition to a business plan is certainly one that outlines a plan to achieve personal development. This plan can be as simple as a list or a series of statements about what you want. Regardless of how you decide to lay out your plan, you should look to discuss your goals in the following areas:

For your business (as per business plan):

- Overall Business Objectives
- Organization Objectives
- Marketing Objectives
- Sales Objectives
- Tracking of your success and activities

Ask yourself what you want to achieve in each of these areas and where you fit into achieving these goals.

For yourself:

- Objectives for personal and family life
- Career objectives
- Financial objectives

The same thing applies here. Look at where you are now and how you feel about each of these areas of your life. You might want to add intellectual/educational objectives to the list and even spiritual objectives but that depends on you. Establish where you are and how you feel at the moment and then look to see what aspects you want to change and can change.

You can get into the habit of doing this for yourself on a regular basis, deciding on the WDYWFY, "What Do You Want For Yourself" points that apply for each year.

Having plans for yourself and your business is the first step to achieving your goals and it will help you affirm your own identity and sense of self for networking purposes. Of course, you need to be open-minded. In a universe of endless possibilities, it's pointless to second guess everything and think there's one way to do everything. There are at least a hundred ways to do most things. So long as you know where you want to go, you're likely to get there.

A classic technique for goal setting and management is SMART.

Specific - Have you clearly defined your goal?

Measurable - How do you know if you are making progress?

Achievable - Is your goal really achievable? Be ambitious but honest.

Rewarding - Is your goal something you are willing to make sacrifices for?

Timely - Is your goal achievable in a meaningful timeframe?

It's used by many of the world's top organizations to assess the nature of their goals. According to the SMART programs, your goals should be:

Set a daily list of action items required to achieve your long-term goals. The steps you take during the first days and the first months may be very simple. The goals may be to read certain books and otherwise gather information that will help you with the achievement of your goals. In the beginning you should work to improve the quality and realism of your goal setting. To stay on track, you should regularly review your plans, and make sure that they continue to fit the way you want to live your life and operate your business.

When you've decided upon your first set of goals, establish a habit to review and update your to-do list on a daily basis. Review your longer-term plans periodically and modify them to reflect your changing priorities and experience.

When it comes to setting your goals, keep this process in mind:

- Write out each goal as a positive statement.
- Be precise when you write your goals, put down dates, times, and amounts so that you can measure your achievement.
- Prioritize your goals because this helps you to avoid feeling overwhelmed and helps to direct your attention to the most important ones.
- Write goals down regularly as this helps you keep them focused and it's a great way to keep them in mind; post

your goals around your home and office space, on the wall, on your door, by the mirror in the bathroom.

- Keep low-level goals you work toward on a daily basis small and achievable in order to give yourself more opportunities for rewarding yourself.

- Take care to set goals in areas where you have control; if you keep your goals focused on your personal performance, you can control whether you achieve them and draw satisfaction from them.

- It is important to set goals that are achievable, in full recognition of your own desires and ambitions.

- Do not set goals too low; the best goals are just slightly out of your immediate grasp, but not so far that there is no hope of achieving them.

As you achieve both your short-term and long-term goals, be sure to enjoy the satisfaction of having done so. Absorb the implications of the goal achievement. Monitor and revel in your progress towards your life goals. Reward yourself. As you start to make good contacts and benefit from then, make sure you're having fun.

Another important exercise is to regularly review your goals. During these reviews you need to check the following:

- Are your goals too easy to achieve? Make your next goals harder.

- Are your goals taking too long to achieve? Make your next set of goals a little easier to achieve.

- Have you learned something that might lead you to change other goals? If the answer is yes, change the relevant goals.
- Have you noticed a deficit in your skills? Set goals to resolve this.

Keep in mind that failure to meet goals does not mean that you are hopeless! As long as you learn from your failures and your mistakes (think of Edison), failure is not an issue. As you learn lessons, incorporate them into your goal-setting program and remember that your goals will change as you mature and grow. Adjust your goals regularly to reflect this growth in your personality. If any one of your goals is no longer attractive to you, let it go and let go of the attached emotions.

Goal setting and reviewing should bring you real pleasure, satisfaction, and a sense of achievement. It should also help you get a handle on the type of people you need to reach out to and how you can use your natural talents to get what you need from a network of contacts.

SKIRTworking, like anything else, is always going to be most effective when you have a definite sense of what you want to achieve from it. If you find yourself wondering one way or another about your achievement with SKIRT™, be prepared first of all to revisit the plan you developed for yourself and see where it has brought you. Modifications may need to be made along the way – but we are proof that this method does work!

CHAPTER FIVE:

Keeping It In The Family

We've already explored why goal setting is imperative for establishing a positive direction for yourself and your business. We hope you're also beginning to understand that a positive outlook is instrumental to ensure successful networking. People respond to positive energy, after all. They don't like to be around people who are insecure or negative, and if you're looking for professionals to do business with, it's highly unlikely you're going to sign up with anyone who is not 110% confident about their own abilities and the strength of their business ideas.

Being positive is not the only consideration when it comes to effective networking, however. You also need to develop the skills to make people feel at home, as well as finding people you can relate to and engage with quickly and effortlessly. Not only does this familial approach help to maintain a positive and warm relationship, it also helps to create a familiarity between contacts that facilitates very effective networking.

Women display their talent for nurturing and networking in familial relationships. A mother is generally on the lookout for opportunities to nurture their children's interests and talents. A sister is perhaps always thinking of how she may help or protect her siblings or benefit from her parents' connections or learn from their mistakes.

We're not saying this behavior is unique to women. It's not. What we are saying, however, is this type of social thinking is a classic feminine characteristic rather than a masculine one. It's a skill that comes more naturally to women than it does to men, whether by nature or nurture. The best we women can do is apply our natural skills and abilities, adapting them to benefit our interests in the business world.

We mentioned in the last chapter that you need to take control and accept that you are the one with the power to change relationships, to build them or not as you see fit. In this chapter, we're going to look at how the actual act of networking effectively resembles managing a household or even a family of relations.

Sherry Thacker, a networking expert, says networking skills are one of the most important life skills a person can master, but that "Women network differently from men [and] like to build relationships and really support one another." Thacker also explains the justification for networking: "You do business with people you know, so you are more likely to take action on a reference or referral from someone you're comfortable with. It's all about trust." You are more likely to take advantage of opportunities that come via someone you know, someone who shares your background, your values, and some of your interests.

A growing number of women are graduating from university and graduate programs these days and headed into top-level management positions. More and more women are also starting their own businesses; records are being set on many fronts and there is growing interest and desire to create word-of-mouth career opportunities for associates and friends. Networking organizations for women have been popping up in response to the demand for these kinds of referrals and opportunities.

Done properly, networking provides an edge and serves as an excellent strategy for gaining career support, professional guidance, and opportunities, as Thacker points out. Collaboration – the sharing of ideas, critical information, and advice – is perfect for promoting business interests.

Interaction with like-minded professionals is invaluable and brings up a key point of networking...keep it in the family. At least initially, you should focus your networking and network building upon people who have a close relationship to you. Not a familial relationship or indeed even a friendly relationship necessarily, but one that is based upon the fact that you have some definite professional interest or experience in common.

Alumni gatherings, conventions, and trade shows are all classic examples of networking events. They bring together people who have something in common (same educational background or same business interests). When you're building your own networking group or looking for a group to join, you need to make sure you are going to make some meaningful contacts. Consider also that you can use professional organizations, industry associations, social clubs, and health clubs for networking as well as specifically designed networking groups.

Getting involved with community organizations is also a great way to get your SKIRT™ network built up. It's altruistic, of course, as an opportunity to give back to your community (an important step when it comes to growing your business), and a great way to expand your reach in terms of people you will interact with. By sitting on the board of organizations or becoming a volunteer leader you not only expand your circle of influence, but you increase your "Googlability", putting your name out there professionally and increasing your general exposure.

Before going any further, let's take a moment to think about the role that the Internet plays in your networking. If you know your way around the World Wide Web (and we will assume most of you do), the concept of search engines is one you're pretty familiar with. There are approximately 1,114,274,426 Internet users out there. (That is nearly one quarter of the world population!) That figure was put forward in 2006 by the Internet World Stat, Miniwatts Marketing Group. You probably use search engines on a regular basis to find what you're looking for online, whether it's Yahoo!®, MSN®, or Google™ that you prefer. A key question in terms of your networking and marketing, however, is how often do you use the Internet to look for yourself and professionals like you?

You don't need an imagination to appreciate why search engines have an important role to play in marketing and indeed networking. Take a second look at the world Internet user statistic and you'll appreciate the overwhelming potential of the medium. The Internet is borderless and largely freeform. If you have access to it through your computer, you have access to millions of people who, although they may not require your services, can nonetheless be an invaluable resource to you in other ways.

If you have a website, you can use the Internet to draw people to you and your business. You can draw clients, yes, but you can also draw potential business partners, mentors, coaches, and more. The key to the Internet: the more people you draw to you online, the more influential you become in the long-run. Even if you use the Internet to chat with professionals in your line of work who operate in a neighboring area, you are still putting yourself and your company out there in a meaningful way, generating word-of-mouth interest for yourself and your business and no doubt enhancing your overall "Googlability".

The thing about search engines and the reason that most online attention is good attention is that people conducting keyword searches rarely go past the first page of results. The more active you are online, the more likely you are to be "googled" and the more likely you are to earn yourself a top search engine ranking. The same can be said for in-real-life activities such as being on boards or otherwise active in your community. Taking part in local charity events should not only help you broaden your outlook as a person and earn some good karma, it should help you get more recognition online and off. These days, newspaper and magazines of all shapes and sizes post articles and other content in online editions; getting your name in the media will also enhance your "Googlability" and your potential for finding network contacts in the future.

If you're planning on joining an already existent networking group, you need to determine whether it's right for you based on your goals. Are you looking to make business contacts, build a support base, or develop your career? Once you can answer this question, you can make more effective choices about which events to attend and which groups to join, not to mention how to organize your own SKIRTworking group when the time comes.

As Thacker points out, "If you are in the wrong group, you are wasting time. Never confuse socializing with networking. If after six months you have not achieved some of your original objectives for joining the group, move on."

Another aspect of staying within a 'family' setting (networking with people who have something in common with you, some relationship), you'll find that word-of-mouth endorsements are key. These are essential to making new contacts and building relationships in an organized manner, which can generate incredible opportunities. Statistics demonstrate, for example, that 50 to 75 percent of job vacancies are unadvertised, part of what is known as the "hidden market". In general, Thacker points out, people referred by business contacts, friends, and relatives tend to fill these hidden jobs.

To effectively network, you've also got to get into the habit of taking an interest in other people and speaking up on their behalf. You need to listen to what they are telling you and be able to ask for what you need, keeping in mind that you're not just talking to them, you are communicating with their entire network. And from your own point of view, you need to be prepared to respond to the information you're being given. The best networkers are genuinely interested in helping their contacts. To get the best results through networking, you should not be out to manipulate or feign interest in order to get what you want. The best networking involves both parties being genuinely engaged and interested in business-based matchmaking.

The best business networkers and the most valuable contacts are well known for their ability to access broad and diverse resources. In many instances, the best networkers can be the "go-to" person when you need anything from a marketing research company to a graphic designer.

According to the wisdom of *Network or Perish: Learn the Secrets of Master Networkers*, some of the most effective ways to find the right network and to get the most out of networking include the following:

- Choosing the right network for your business
- Visiting organization meetings at least twice before joining the group as joining can be expensive
- Being prepared to commit to events
- Getting involved (perhaps volunteering to be on a committee or doing a job during the meeting itself)
- Always presenting a positive image
- Handing out business cards
- Scheduling follow-up meetings with prospective contacts
- Appearing confident at all times
- Using body language to present a positive and professional image
- Being proactive and introducing yourself first
- Having a good hand-shake

- Using a person's name several times when you first meet
- Having some questions planned
- Listening intently

Networking through your own SKIRT™ Network is likely to help you perfect these networking techniques by being around professional women who not only share your interests in developing strong business contacts but also your innate ability to network and nurture in a familial way.

CHAPTER SIX:
Calendered Contacts

A s you begin to familiarize yourself with the actual process of meeting and greeting business contacts, you're likely to find yourself running into problems in terms of follow-up. It's one of the biggest challenges individuals experience when it comes to networking. Most people start networking with no clear idea of what they want to achieve and with the firm belief that they are going to see immediate gains when they start engaging in a networking group. Immediate gains and favorable results in networking are not feasible in the vast majority of situations. On top of that, you are networking for all the wrong reasons if you are trying to get a quick-fix solution to your present situation.

In networking, you should strive for long-term gains. You're forming relationships, as we suggested in the chapter about "keeping it in the family". Your networking contacts are very likely to be people you are friendly with, people you invite to dinner, who you brainstorm with over a cup of coffee and send a personalized card to at Christmas. Networking contacts are not the type of people you are going to meet once and then be done with. It's in your best interest to cultivate a deep relationship. You don't have to become best friends with everyone you ever sit down to discuss business with, but you do have to keep their name, number, address, and e-mail handy so that you can check in with them on a regular basis.

Many people also make the mistake of thinking that the size of a networking group is the most significant detail when they look into this particular networking approach. Although people will start to worry when groups start to fall in size, the number of participants really has very little to do with how effective a networking group is. You may well be part of a networking group that has only two or three members at some point. What you'll find, though, is that in such a small group, it is particularly easy for members to draw benefit from the relationship. Focus on quality rather than quantity.

You also have to stop thinking about how many leads you haven't got and focus on how many leads you've actually given out, or the number of effective suggestions you've made to contacts with issues relating to their business. It can also be an important part of the process to call contacts and offer a simple compliment, preferably about their business. You've got to put in the time and effort to help people feel comfortable offering you a referral. Their credibility with their contact is certainly at stake when they put you in touch with people they know.

If you find yourself at a business event, running around, going from person to person, with the expectations of first giving them your business card and hoping to get theirs, you're far too unorganized in your approach and you're certainly not going to be building a relationship with a person. Networking groups that make a game out of collecting business cards to see who can collect the most in a given time period, well, they're just wasting good business cards!

The best networkers are like good tennis players. They're always on their toes and they always have a game plan. They are often highly effective at networking because they work the net and keep a particular goal in mind. One of the most effective goals is to meet and have meaningful discussions with only three people at each event.

Once a business networking event is over, the real relationship building begins. Your goal should be to attend the networking event to meet and build rapport but you need to schedule a follow-up within 24 hours. Send a personalized card to the contact and call a few days later to arrange a time to meet for a coffee or to have lunch. Find out in a relaxed setting exactly what you can do for the contact and their business.

Ideally you're going to establish a schedule to organize your networking activities, ensuring that you have a high conversion rate for opportunities.

CHAPTER SEVEN:
The Ladies Who Lunch

Okay, so who are the ladies who lunch? In this instance, we're referring to women in business or on a career path who want to build networks of contacts. For the purposes of this chapter, consider yourself a lady who does lunch. If you don't already, you're going to start!

As you begin to draw together ideas about networking, you should begin to develop clear goals in regards to what you want to achieve by networking and why. You're also going to realize the importance of impressions – first impressions in particular – as you begin to meet and greet other businesswomen.

First of all, you need to think about who you want to 'show up as'. Almost without exception, you're going to be evaluated within the first three seconds of a new encounter based on your appearance and any visible mannerisms; based on what you're saying and doing.

People will assess your visual and behavioral appearance, giving you the complete once-over. They will check out your demeanor, mannerisms, and body language. Women, in particular, will even assess your appearance (clothes, etc.) and accessories – watch, handbag, briefcase. The impression you make may be indelible, intriguing to some and, inevitably, disenchanting to others.

Prepare yourself to make a good first impression with just about everyone you meet by being aware of how the process works. Nine times out of ten, it works something like this:

People will look at how you fit in the context of a particular business or social level. If you appear comfortable in a particular setting, you are considered suitable for further interaction.

When you appear to belong to a higher business or social level than the general one you are in, most people will admire you and look to you as a valuable contact.

If you appear to be of lower business or social status, it's likely you'll only be tolerated. Most people will keep you at a distance and largely write you off (obviously avoid this one!).

The process is very much like an interview situation and you should, in essence, treat your networking efforts as such. Also, try not to feel too uncomfortable about it. Instead, recognize that it is human nature to constantly make these appraisals. You do it, too, without question, whether it's in a business or a social environment. If you met someone for the first time in their work out clothes jogging down the street you might have a different impression of them than if you had met the same person in an Armani suit at a restaurant. Same person, different impression. The first impression registers in your brain and constitutes an immediate initial assessment. Go with the flow and learn to make a positive and lasting first impression at every networking function, in every networking situation. Modify your approach as necessary to suit any situation and with a bit of practice, you will always come out on top, often with a few good contacts to show for it. A good first impression has a lot to do with how you feel about yourself and your life in general, as odd as it may seem. You'll need to regularly assess your personality, physical appearance, overall health, lifestyle, and goals, not to mention work on them regularly as we discussed in the earlier chapter on goal-setting.

If you make a good impression, you're not necessarily through the door; you probably have a foot wedged in but you're not yet a member of the club. If you happen to know any former society ladies – perhaps you have a distant relative who enjoyed her afternoon teas – you know it takes more than a smile and a handshake to be accepted. This is very much the same in business, particularly when you're doing business in the hope of securing referrals.

Imagine it. If you worked with a professional in a field closely related to your own, you'd not only have a pretty good knowledge of what they should be doing as part of their job, you'd also have pretty clear expectations of how they should be doing their job. A nurse or physiotherapist may have a very different job description compared to a surgeon, but if all three worked in the same hospital department, they more than likely can assess each other's work and make a determination as to whether they each are competent at their job. To make the determination, however, it's important to have more than a first impression to go on.

The situation is similar in most areas of business and it does indeed bear a resemblance to the attitude of the higher echelons of society. You're not a member of the club until you've proven your worth.

The most important detail when it comes to establishing yourself: you have to show you can go above and beyond the immediate requirements. Good customer service is about anticipating the needs of clients and addressing them very quickly. When you're bidding for a referral, it's important to show you're on the ball when you speak with your potential referrer, your network connecter.

Let's assume you're the one organizing a professional lunch meeting to further your business interests. First and foremost, you need to ensure you are meeting with the right type of person. Just as you are sized up, you need to scrutinize the people you seek out and interact with. Particularly if you're organizing the meeting, you should be on time (first rule: punctuality), you should also have basic information to hand out to your lunch partner. You should have general information about their business experience, their educational background, and their business objectives. If possible, and particularly for first meetings (in case you need to break the ice), you should also seek out a few personal/family details (whether they're married, how many kids they have, that sort of thing). Appreciating the importance of this information is another factor that makes women good networkers; it's a personal approach that helps people feel that they are being valued.

The type of women you should be sitting down to lunch with are smart, creative thinkers. They should have a proven track record in their industry, one that you can verify with a simple Google™ search or a conversation with "the right people". They should be go-getters who operate in an industry related to your own, not too many degrees of separation, that is.

Once you're at the table, your focus needs to be on directing the conversation toward a collaborative business venture. A few items you should clarify for yourself before you even think about making a meeting with another professional include knowing your immediate and long-term business needs that you can address with the help of another professional. If you are looking for more clients, think about precisely what type of clients you're looking for (those who have small projects but regular work, perhaps, or those who might only require your services once or twice a year but each time will have a lot of work for you to do). What can your schedule handle? Are you looking to get a few high-profile clients to increase your "Googlability"? You might also be looking to hire someone to help you with your business, in which case you should have a clear idea of the type of professional you're looking to hire before you even set the date for your lunch meeting.

Necessity may be the mother of invention but preparation is the father of inspiration; preparation for the all-important lunch meeting will result in you getting exactly what you need and want. The more often you organize social lunches with one or more professional women, the more adept you will become at identifying and working toward the realization of particular business opportunities. What's more, you're going to find that you meet many great ladies to lunch with at your local SKIRT™ Network.

Always begin a lunch by seeking to understand the other person's business, what motivates them and how you can help and support them. Then you can address how collaborating is in the best interest for the both of you. You can then tie that in to what you do and what you are looking for. End the lunch with specific next steps and be sure to follow up on them!

CHAPTER EIGHT:

How To Start Your Own SKIRT™ Network

A re you ready to get started? As the founder of your SKIRT™ Network, the first item on your action list should be to identify the scope of your network. The average person has approximately 400 to 500 friends, acquaintances, and relationships. That seems like a large number but when the Financial Planner thought about it, between the Financial Womens' Association (550 members), her client base (200), her happy hour list (150), her graduating class of high school (150), and the other advisors in Northern California (250) that already brings the total count up to over 1,000! If you have 10 people in your SKIRT™ group, that is nearly 10,000 contacts. From that number everyone could get enough business to keep them successful! A great exercise at one of your first SKIRT™ meetings (or before you invite someone to join your group) is to do a brainstorming session to figure out how large of a scope your network is. Some questions to ask are:

- How many people do you know in your church, club, or charity?
- Do you have children that go to school?
- Do your children belong to any sports teams or out of school activities?
- Do you belong to a trade association?
- How many people are there in your immediate or extended family?
- How many people in your neighborhood do you know on a first name basis?
- If you were to host a party, how many people would you invite?
- How many clients do you have?
- How many professionals do you consistently use? (CPA, attorneys, plumbers, dentists, doctors, architects, etc.)
- How many organization presidents do you know?
- Do you have any business colleagues, employees, peers?
- Are there wholesalers that call on you?
- Are you involved with any sports teams, book clubs, etc?
- Do you volunteer?

After you have created a list of potential members you can now create your SKIRT™ Network.

We have developed a checklist to ensure that starting your SKIRT™ Network is as easy as 1-2-3.

1. Create a leadership board.

2. Plan a leadership kick-off meeting.
- Create a name for your group
- Create a mission statement you can work with
- Assign leadership roles
- Determine who you want to join from your sphere of influence
- Determine day, time, and venue of monthly meeting that will work for your members
- Set the first meeting date
- Send invites to members with next meeting information (2 weeks before meeting)
- Set up a website for your group

3. Plan your first group meeting.
- Describe purpose of group
- Have one leadership person describe their business
- Draw names for presentations/hospitality for the rest of the year
- Discuss first member networking event
- From the second meeting on you can follow the sample agendas

Building your own SKIRT™ Network really is this simple. You can get it going in three easy steps. Do not try to recreate the wheel. Do as we did. Identify two professionals that you know, trust and like and invite them to sit on your leadership board. When considering co-founders for your group, be sure they have the following characteristics:

1. Reliability
2. Professionalism
3. Understanding of referrals
4. A desire to grow their business - do they show it
5. A definitive target market
6. A large network
7. Common goals

Creating a Leadership Board

Your SKIRT™ Network will only be as good as its leadership board. Your leadership board makes all group decisions, that is why it is important to find committed and organized individuals to run the show. In our group, the Leadership team meets separately on a monthly basis to discuss pending issues.

We suggest a Leadership Board that rotates on a pre-determined basis. The main roles include:

1. Meeting Leader/Moderator
2. Membership Chair - Application
3. Secretary
4. Treasurer

The tasks should be defined as follows:

Meeting Leader/Moderator:

1. Prepares the agenda and brings copies to the monthly meeting.
2. Keeps the meeting on track. (We suggest a timer.)
3. Sends the monthly reminder. (We use www.evite.com.)

Membership Chair:

1. Fields all questions in regards to membership.
2. Accepts applications.
3. Speaks with applicants to discuss membership.
4. Discusses the application with the Leadership Board.
5. Secures the signed Commitment Form.

Secretary:

1. Adds the new members to the roster and website.
2. Takes notes at meeting and uploads onto the website.
3. Uploads presentations to the website.
4. Prepares the annual calendar of speakers and events.

Treasurer:

1. Collects money for special events.

For every monthly meeting there is also a presenter. Their duties are as follows:

1. Makes a 30 minute presentation.
2. Brings refreshments.
3. Prepares any handouts specific to their topic.

For your first Leadership Board meeting, ask your Board Leaders to prepare and bring a list of potential members they know and trust and who they think would enhance your referral-based networking group. Consider also those who you believe will be able to consistently attend, but more importantly, who will positively contribute to your monthly meetings. When writing this list of potential SKIRT™ members, remember the most likely membership candidates will be either self-employed or work at a company within which they were charged with building their own book of business. Give some consideration to the people you know whose business profiles will naturally cause referrals to your business but remember that SKIRT™ is also about developing referrals from existing resources, i.e., people that are already in your circle of influence or people in business for themselves that you just know and like. Below is a list of occupations or business verticals that we established as the core group for the SKIRT™ network. In our group, we have had as many as 27 women, and do not recommend your group consist of more than 30. If the group is too large, when everyone is present, it becomes too lively to manage. At any one time, there is only one person in each business category. This approach eliminates any awkwardness between members in the same business category, if the one member is referred and not the other.

Here's a list of sample business categories that comprise our SKIRT™ Network:

Professions for SKIRT™ Network

Real Estate Agent	Rental Broker	Doctor
Mortgage Broker	Professional Recruiter	Marketing Consultant
Financial Planner	Family Law Attorney	Photographer
Certified Professional Accountant	Life Coach	Website Designer
1031 Exchange Professional	Therapist	Art Gallery Owner
Estate Planning Attorney	Company Payroll Representative	Boutique/Store Owner
Landscape Architect	Personal Trainer	Restaurant/ bar owner
Architect	Pilates /Yoga Instructor	Caterer
Interior Designer	Dentist	Wine Sales Representative
Insurance Agent	Hairdresser	Plastic Surgeon

Your own core group may be different, but the point is to create the list and start from there.

This SKIRT™ Network was originally set up as a way for business owners to build their business by generating referrals. Yet over time, many other benefits have been recognized. The women who join a group such as this should be interested in the following:

1. Building their business through referrals.
2. Supporting other women in building their businesses through referrals.
3. Building a 'dream team' of trustworthy professional women to help their own clients.
4. Having a support network.
5. Having a board of directors at their fingertips to ask for business advice.
6. Finding out firsthand what their target market thinks.
7. Learning: Though we all come from different professions, we all have the same concerns as business owners and can learn from what our peers are doing.
8. Accountability: All members are accountable for their goals.
9. Having a forum to share challenges and successes!

What members are saying about SKIRT™:

"SKIRT™ has become an important referral resource for me. But, more importantly, it is a sounding board when I need honest feedback on a variety of issues. I know I can rely on the professionalism and the basic integrity and good judgment of other members."

A SKIRT™ member

"Unlike other networking groups, SKIRT™ members represent a broad range of professions and careers. Therefore, I have had the opportunity of meeting people I might not otherwise encounter in my daily life. At our meetings we educate each other about our respective businesses and discuss current business concerns. But the best part of our meetings is the informal round table discussion which provides a friendly forum for the members to solicit help with work-related problems or challenges they may be facing."

A SKIRT™ member

"SKIRT™ has created for me a comfortable space to unfold the possibilities that lie ahead of me, within both my professional endeavors and my personal ones. In sharing even a brief window each month of my recent highlights and upcoming plans, I am able to appreciate the time and look ahead. Whatever uncertainties I may show up with about my direction and choices I made with my career, I continually receive support, guidance and strength from the women in the group. And all I did was show up. Thank you for creating this amazing roundtable of women."

A SKIRT™ member

SKIRT™ has given me the opportunity to align myself with some of the most dynamic, powerful, and motivating women in my community. SKIRT™ has helped me grow both personally and professionally, and I feel fortunate to work with such fabulous women!

* Samantha Strickler, Strickler Insurance

Developing your Mission Statement

When creating the SKIRT™ Network, we thought it was important to develop a Mission Statement so that our group could stay focused on the meaning of SKIRT™ and why they joined. When we all sat down to share our thoughts on this exercise, we realized that our mission is quite simply the name of our group!

SKIRT™ Mission Statement

Sharing Knowledge, Information and Resources Together!

At each of meetings, our Mission Statement is displayed on an easel and referred to often to remind us why we are there.

Processing Membership Applications

Once the word is out about your SKIRT™ Network, you will be inundated with requests from women wanting to join. Be prepared and have a process in place so that it flows nicely and does not cause a drain on your time. Ask one of your Leadership Board members to be the Membership Chair to take charge of this aspect of your network. At our Leadership Board Kick-off meeting, we identified the following process for accepting memberships and it has worked well for our SKIRT™ Network.

1. The candidate member will submit a Membership Application Form (go to www.skirtworking.com to download), with a personal biography or resume to the Membership Chair.

2. After receiving the Membership Application Form, the Membership Chair contacts the applicant for a brief phone or in-person interview to discuss what the membership entails and seeks to understand why the candidate is interested in SKIRT™ Network. The Membership Chair will ask why the candidate feels she can provide a meaningful contribution to the other group members. She will then review the SKIRT Commitment Form™ and the SKIRT 11 Commandments™. Note: It is important to discuss each line of the Commitment Form™ and why it exists (no matter how obvious each point seems) with each prospective member.

3. At the monthly Leadership Board meetings, the Membership Chair will present all new member applications to the other board members for review and approval.

4. If approved, the Membership Chair extends an offer to the candidate member, in the form of a letter, which requests the new member sign and return The Commitment Form™.

5. The new member contact details are then added to the website and an email notification is circulated to introduce the new member to the other SKIRT™ Network members.

6. The new member is formally presented at the next monthly meeting.

The SKIRT 11 Commandments™

1. Skirts optional!

2. Set goals and share them.

3. Celebrate successes.

4. Do what you say you are going to do. (Follow through!)

5. Treat your referrals the way you want your clients to be treated!

6. Be on time.

7. Ask questions and listen closely to the answers.

8. Develop meaningful professional relationships.

9. Be a trusted resource.

10. Serve your clients and SKIRT™ Network members.

11. Tell everyone what you do.

Running and Managing your Meetings

Thus far we have focused on the subject of leading your SKIRT™ Network with the creation of a leadership board. It is important, however, to determine how you will lead the meetings. The management of the meeting should be discussed at your Leadership Board Kick-Off. We have learned that meetings are best kept to two hours at a maximum to keep member's attention and to ensure efficiency.

We have also learned that as the group grows and the members develop friendships, it becomes increasingly difficult to keep the meeting on track. Therefore, developing an agenda for your meetings is an important component of the success of your SKIRT™ Network. At our Leadership Board Kick-Off meeting, we developed a standard template for the agenda that would be used for each meeting with the knowledge that the format and contents of the meeting agenda might change over time as we learned more about our members' needs.

You will notice from the Commitment Form™ that we ask each member to have read the meeting agenda ahead of time. This is so that no time is wasted on answering questions about what is on the agenda at our monthly meetings.

SKIRT™ Network Meeting
AGENDA

Meeting Date: *[Insert Mtg Date]*

Meeting Moderator: *[Alternate monthly between*
                                        Leadership Board Members]

Meeting Time: 6:00 pm – 8:00 pm

Tonight's Sponsor
& Presenter: *[Name of Member]*
                                        [Member's company Name]

6:00 – 6:30: Hospitality Reception & Acknowledgments

This session lasts for ½ hour and is an opportunity for everyone to catch up and to decompress after a hard day of work. The meeting's sponsor/presenter is responsible for bringing the light food, wine and sodas to be enjoyed in the Hospitality session. The Meeting Moderator brings the session to a close and thanks the sponsor/presenter for providing the refreshments.

6:30 – 6:50: Member Update & News

In this 20 minute session, the Meeting Moderator provides a 1 minute introduction of any new member to the organization (or any guest who has joined the meeting for the purpose of evaluating the Network). This is followed by an around the table update from each member. Each member should have 1- 3 minutes (depending upon the number of members present) to update the group on their situation since the last meeting. This update can be personal, professional or otherwise.

6:50 – 7:20: Member Presentation

In this 30 minute session, one group member describes her company, her ideal client and how the other SKIRT members can help her develop her client base. (The presenter is encouraged to prepare a hand out summarizing their presentation for the other group members to take home.)

7:20 – 7:30: New Business

During this session, the Meeting Moderator will announce the Sponsor/ Presenter for the next meeting, the details of the next SKIRT™ Group Social Event and any other matters that the Leadership Board would like to mention. The Group will also be asked if there are any matters that they feel need to be addressed.

7:30 – 7:50: Group Break-Out Session

This 20 minute session allows group members to break out into groups of two, in one-on-one sessions, to learn how they can each help each other. Members should endeavor to talk to a different person at each meeting.

7:50 – 8:00: Referral Victories

In closing out the meeting, this 10 minute session allows for each member to share their referral victory stories and to thank other members for their referrals.

DATE OF NEXT MEETING:

[Insert Date of Next Meeting]

Next Month's Sponsor/Presenter:

[Insert Name & Company Name of Next Month's Sponsor/Presenter]

(An Actual Agenda from our April 6th, 2006 Meeting)

SKIRT™ Meeting
AGENDA

Meeting Date: April 6th, 2006

Meeting Moderator: Michelle Balog, Real Estate Broker

Meeting Time: 6:00 pm – 8:00 pm

Tonight's Sponsor & Presenter: Michelle Alberda, XYZ Financial

6:00 – 6:30: Hospitality Reception & Acknowledgments

(Thank you to Michelle Balog for moderating this evening's meeting and to Michelle Alberda, tonight's presenter, for providing both the refreshments and the venue!)

6:30 – 6:50: Member Update & News

New member introduction – Welcome to Jane Doe, President and Founder of Do It Yourself Pilates

Around the table member update - 1 minute each member, max

6:50 – 7:20: Member Presentation

Michelle Alberda will describe her Ideal Client as a Financial Planner and how we as a group can help her develop her client base through referrals. (See Michelle's Hand Out).

7:20 – 7:30: New Business

Review of 2006 Group Meeting Presenter List: May's Presenter & Sponsor is Stacey Fleece (May 5th, 2006)

Save the Date: June's Member Networking Event is sponsored by The Hair Salon and will be held on June 15th 6:00pm – 8:00pm. RSVP for yourself and your guests to the Hairdresser by no later than May 1.

Member Issues: Ladies - Anything to report or discuss?

7:30 – 7:50: Group Break Out Session

Break out into groups of two- how can we help each other?

7:50 – 8:00: Referral Victories

Around the table announcement of referral victories.

DATE OF NEXT MEETING:

Thursday May 5th, 2006

NEXT MONTH'S MEETING SPONSOR/PRESENTER:

Stacey Fleece

Presenter List

As we are all very busy businesswomen, planning ahead is key. Our SKIRT™ meeting is the 2nd Thursday of every month at the Financial Planner's office. As mentioned previously, the presenter brings the refreshments. At the 1st meeting of the year, we draw names for hospitality and publish the list. If it turns out that the presenter cannot make it - that person must find a replacement.

2006 Sample Presenter List	
Month	**Presenter**
January	New Year Goal Sharing
February	The Payroll Representative
March	The Architect
April	Real Estate Agent
May	Financial Planner
June	Spa Party
July	The Hairdresser
August	Goal check-in
September	Estate Planning Attorney
October	Mortgage Broker
November	Pilates Instructor
December	Holiday Party

Presenter Hand-Out

It is next to impossible to refer people if you do not understand what they do. That is why the first round of presentations is for each SKIRT™ network member to have thirty minutes to explain who they are, what they do, and their ideal client. Below is an example of the 'ideal client' letter Michelle presented to the group. She gave each member a copy of the letter so that they could refer back to it.

Referring potential clients to Michelle Alberda,
Certified Financial Planner© certificant

In order to facilitate referrals, I have described my
'ideal' client below. I have also included a description
of 'life events' where my help can prove invaluable.

My ideal client is a single woman or a woman that
is the financial decision maker in her family/domestic
partnership. Smart money management is the family's main
financial goal. Their household income is over $200,000
per year and they have investable assets exceeding
$500,000. They desire comprehensive ongoing financial
planning and assistance with asset management.

Life triggers:
  Divorce
  Inheritance
  Rental Real Estate Sale
  Second Home Sale
  Transition to a "retirement community", selling primary
  residence
  New home purchase
  Combining households, second marriage
  Job transition
  Job changes, unmanaged prior company 401(k)s
  Unhappy with portfolio return/service
  Excess cash in the bank/money market/savings
  account
  Stock option exercise
  IRA transfer
  401(k) rollover
  Newly self-employed

I have included a welcome folder for any client that
you refer to me that briefly explains the value that I
can add as their Chief Financial Officer.

Michelle Alberda, CFP©
Senior Financial Advisor

Once all of our members had the opportunity to introduce their businesses to our group, we exchanged the agenda item on introductions to other topics. Here are a few examples of other topics. Additional topics can be found on our website: www.skirtworking.com.

SKIRT™ meeting 30 minute topics

1. Business planning – including mission, vision, numbers, etc.
2. Exercise to determine size of member's contact base
3. How to give referrals.
4. Holiday/networking party for members.
5. Holiday/networking party for non-members.
6. Each member come prepared with a problem, obstacle, information, presentation.
7. Fees.
8. Staffing.
9. Life balance.
10. Marketing and PR.
11. Book review.
12. Brainstorming sessions (ways to thank clients for referrals, ways to get more referrals, etc.)

Member Networking Events

Networking and relationship building events within the group are important. As some individuals have never utilized each other's services, it is important to have the opportunity to get to know each other and to further develop trust. The first December we held a holiday party at the co-founder's house. Everyone brought a bottle of wine and the caterer in the group made the food and the cost was divided. This was a great opportunity to experience the caterer's services and to develop bonds in a more natural setting. The next semi-annual event was held at the spa where the hairdresser works. Everyone brought wine and the spa supplied the fruit, cheese and crackers. Those who wanted services (massages, facials, manicures, etc.) paid for their own and the others sat around the fireplace in their robes and caught up! In both instances the members commented on how nice it was to have the opportunity to bond in a less structured (no agenda!!!) environment.

Showing Appreciation

Another principle of referrals is that we are not owed referrals, we earn them. When one receives a referral, it is a gift, it is not a requirement. In our group we have a 10 minute session when we thank each other for referrals. We do not "keep score" but it is important to share these "referral victories". We recommend that you provide a referral tracker (this can be found at www.skirtworking.com) to your members and collect them at each meeting.

It is important to acknowledge the person that gave the referral for several reasons.

1. The referrer wants to know the status of the referral.

2. The referrer is not required to give the referral – it is a gift. We all know that we give thanks when we receive a gift.

3. If it does not seem that the referee is excited about their referral – they may not receive them anymore.

In our group, a thank you can come in many forms. It could be verbal, it could be an email thank you, it could be a gift card, or it could be a referral that comes back from another direction. The biggest thank you comes in knowing that the person we are sending to a fellow SKIRT™ member will get the best possible professional service.

Within the SKIRT™ Network, a verbal or written thank you is more than sufficient. However, for people outside our network who send us referrals, it is important to go the extra mile. AT A MINIMUM, one should send a thank you email or make a phone call. Preferably, you should send a hand written note. Other great ideas include:

- Buying a table at a gala, luncheon or charity event (preferably one that you or your referral champions support) and invite your friends/family/colleagues/networking group members who send you the most referrals.

- Throwing a black tie event and invite only those who sent you referrals in the last year.

- Taking the person who referred you out for a meal with the person they referred!

- Throwing a party for the people who referred new clients to you and have them bring someone else they would like to introduce to you.

- Sending a nice gift- a bottle of wine, flowers, a gift card if you don't know what they like, something useful for their favorite hobby, handmade cookies, etc. Go the extra mile and send it to their office so they can share it with those in their office.

Whatever you do, it is important that the people you thank know why they are being thanked so they will send you more referrals!

Referral Gone Wrong

Unfortunately, whenever there is human interaction, there is the possibility that something will go wrong. It is inevitable. It is not a question of "if" but "when". Make sure your group has a way of dealing with referrals that go wrong. This should be addressed on the commitment form or in the initial interview process. In the instance that someone refers a potential client to a SKIRT™ Network member and the referral ends up having a problem with that member, that member should be advised. It would be difficult to hear, but that member would rather hear it than not get additional referrals. It could be a personality clash but it could also be that a member of the group acted inappropriately. If it is the latter, then that person needs to be removed from the group. If it is a personality clash – and that is bound to happen at some point – it is important that someone (the membership leader) have a discussion with the SKIRT member to determine the best course of action.

The Website

Once a potential member has been officially invited to join our SKIRT™ Network, we add them to our SKIRT™ website. (www. skirtnetwork.net.) All members have their biography, a photo and contact information readily accessible on this site for marketing purposes. Many of us have added this link in the footer of our outgoing emails as yet another way to generate referrals. Having all of the members' information on one site has many advantages:

1. No need to carry the other members' cards.
2. Everyone's information is current.
3. It saves trees!
4. Potential clients can easily find information on the 'dream team'.
5. Another opportunity to show up on a search engine!

This is it in a nutshell! Does it seem like a lot of work? Or, does it seem too simple to be effective? Believe us, it works. We know from three years of experience and figuring it out along the way. Don't create more work than you need to. Find a strategy that works and stick to it! As previously stated, SKIRTworking may not pay off tomorrow but it will create unlimited referrals soon! At some point you may feel frustrated and think that this isn't working for you. Never fear, contact us at skirtworking.com to find frequently asked questions and solutions. There are slight nuances that can make or break the success of your group and any issues can be resolved.

CHAPTER NINE

Implementing SKIRT™ Strategies In Your Business

t SKIRT™ group, we have created numerous strategies to refer business to each other. Now that you have a clear idea about how you can go about building your own SKIRT™ Network, it's time for us to share our strategies to help your group achieve its full potential.

The Shortest Distance Referral

This is the most common SKIRT™ referral....directly from one member to another. One member has a client that needs a particular service, there is another member in the group that offers that exact service, and voila....client is sent from point A to point B.

A simple example of this is a client "toss" from the Financial Planner to the Mortgage Broker. The Financial Planner met with clients that wanted to review their finances with her because they were in interested in buying a house. The Financial Planner immediately picked up the phone during their meeting, called the Mortgage Broker, and an appointment was set with the clients and the mortgage broker for the following evening to discuss mortgage options. It doesn't get much easier or cost effective than that!

The Boomerang Referral

Sometimes a member of the group will meet with a potential client and at that first meeting find the client needs the services of another member in the group. The referral from one member to another is made before the original person is even an official client of the "referrer." In this case, sometimes it is the "referee" that ends up referring the client back to the original member.... much like a boomerang.

Case in point – the Real Estate Agent met with potential clients who were interested in buying their first home. She referred them to the Mortgage Broker to run some numbers for them and get them preapproved for financing. This was all done in short order....but then the clients decided to take a back seat in the housing market. Six months later, they stumbled on a condominium that they were very interested in and came back to the Mortgage Broker to revisit payment numbers. They had lost touch with the Real Estate Agent by this point and now didn't have an agent. The Mortgage Broker was able to refer them back to the Real Estate Agent.... the original point of contact...and the two of them ended up completing the deal!

The Referral That Keeps on Giving

This is otherwise known as the multi-generational referral. This referral really goes to the heart of how being involved in a SKIRT™ Network is just smart business. It is not only about the other SKIRT™ members you meet with once a month but rather the reach of THEIR spheres of influence. Here's how it works: the Financial Planner received a referral from the Real Estate Agent with whom the Mortgage Broker had worked on a deal. That Real Estate Agent referred a colleague of hers to the Financial Planner. From there, the Financial Planner received a referral to a client of the colleague....and so on, and so on, and so on.

The Triple Play

Often times, when your SKIRT™ Network gets large and represents quite a few different services, opportunities arise to refer a client to more than one member at a time. These multiple member referrals are not always going to be in the same combination – it is important to listen closely to your client and hear what their needs are. Often times, the client doesn't even know where his or her needs lie and in your role as trusted advisor, you are able to navigate efficiently.

The Mortgage Broker had clients that she had preapproved for real estate financing and these clients had been working with a real estate agent in San Francisco County. The clients ended up poking around real estate in Marin County and found a place they were interested in but didn't know if they could afford it. Since they were currently working with an agent based in San Francisco County, they needed representation in Marin. The Mortgage Broker was able to refer them to a Marin real estate agent to represent them on the property and then was able to refer them to the CPA to review tax benefits of this pending purchase and the Financial Planner to help them understand the future financial implications of the purchase. The dream team in action!

The Backhand Referral

Going back to the "sometimes clients don't know what they actually need" concept, often times referrals are given indirectly through alternative means. During conversation, a client may subtly express a need but not ask specifically for advice…but then in the course of asking for help in a different arena, the member is able to direct them where they really needed to be in the first place.

For example, the Hairdresser had a client come into her chair for a cut and color. During their discussion, the client told the Hairdresser that she was considering buying a home in the San Francisco area (she was from Boston) but never asked the Hairdresser for recommendations or referrals and didn't seem to indicate she needed or wanted that. However, later in the same discussion, this client asked the Hairdresser if she knew of any good plastic surgeons. The hairdresser knew that the Mortgage Broker had a good friend who was a plastic surgeon so gave her client the Mortgage Broker's card and told her to call and get the information from the Mortgage Broker. She also subtly mentioned to the client that the Mortgage Broker could help her on her potential San Francisco home purchase. Everyone wins!

Grab the Spotlight Referral

Another efficient method of attaining referrals is if someone can get a speaking engagement that allows them to present to a larger group of possible clients and/or referral sources. In some instances, members of your SKIRT™ Network can recommend other members to be "experts" on certain topics for business presentations or panels.

Several examples of this type of referral have worked within our group recently. We have a family law attorney that, in her practice, deals with divorces. Usually when there is a divorce, one party has to buy the other party out of a home or they have to sell and both buy new places, etc. The attorney in our SKIRT™ Network belongs to an industry group of family law attorneys that are often looking for speakers for lunch programs. She was able to invite the mortgage broker to present at a lunch program to a room of 30+ family law attorneys – all of whom have the potential to be referral sources for the Mortgage Broker.

The Real Estate Agent's office has a weekly meeting with all the real estate agents that work in her company. They, too, have weekly speakers and are always looking for new topics. The Real Estate Agent was able to get one of our members who does payroll for small businesses on the agenda one week. Since most real estate agents are incorporated as small businesses that need payroll service, it was a great captive audience for her.

For some types of business categories within your SKIRT™ Network, where there is a strong correlation and opportunity to refer business among one another, you can hold an event where your clients glean information on a topic they are interested in and you provide the experts! We (the authors – a financial planner, a real estate agent and a mortgage broker) have found this type of event to be extremely fruitful in yielding new clients, as well as helping existing clients. Our first such event was targeted towards our potential homeowner clients. Many of the Financial Planner's clients, who utilized her financial planning services, were renters interested in getting on the property ladder as part of their strategy to build wealth. As first time home buyers however, many were uncertain as to how to begin the process. The Financial Planner found that having the same conversation with multiple clients on a one-on-one basis was not only a drain on her time but also created a road block for her clients because they had to go and seek information, individually, from all the different players who would facilitate the deal of purchasing real estate. Basically, they either did not have the time to do it or were fearful to jump in. The Financial Planner's solution was to set up a discussion panel event entitled "How to Buy Real Estate." Three of each of the pertinent players who help bring together a real estate deal were invited to sit on the panel – three mortgage brokers, three real estate agents and three CPAs. The Financial Planner acted as the moderator to facilitate the flow of information and to explain how each of the processes works together. The event was marketed not only to all of her clients, but also to clients and friends of the all the panelists. The concept was simple and the event turned out to be a wild success. Standing room only in fact!

The event was held after work and advertised that food, wine and soft drinks would be provided. This was to ensure we didn't lose any potential attendees during the hungry hour! The Financial Planner began the event by asking a set of frequently asked questions developed ahead of time by each of the panelists and then opened the floor up to questions. The format was perfect because all of the attendees fed off each other's questions and afterwards, each of the panelists were able to circulate around the room and speak to people individually. The audience appreciated it because they were able to personally "interview" three mortgage brokers and three real estate agents and they were able to find one from each category with whom they were able to work. The Financial Planner was especially thrilled. "Not only was I able to provide a value added service for my clients through holding the event, I was also able to get the panelists to cover the cost to rent the room and the refreshments so it was nothing out of pocket for me. The panelists were thrilled because it was an easy way to get in front of 70 potential clients! It was a win-win." This event could be modified for the various SKIRT™ members to provide various benefits to all involved!

The Spend a Day in My Chair Referral

One great way to facilitate the referral process is an idea that came from the Financial Planner. As a financial planner, she frequently comes across clients who do not have their estate planning done. This is not good – particularly when clients have children. She gives her clients the names of three different estate planning attorneys so they can interview and choose one with whom they want to work. More often than not, clients do not follow through as they are too busy in their everyday life to take care of this. The Financial Planner solved this problem by scheduling a day each quarter with a different estate planning attorney and suggested to her clients that if they wanted to work with attorney 'x' they could come into her office that day and she would be able to sit in on the meeting with them. The Financial Planner's clients loved this idea for many reasons:

1. The Financial Planner, a familiar and friendly face, is able to make all the introductions, provide the background information, and set the stage for what can often times be an uncomfortable and awkward meeting.

2. Her office is familiar territory for her clients and they feel comfortable there.

3. At any given time, the Financial Planner can provide any and all relevant financial information that would be requested in the meeting.

4. Most people like to work with a referral. It offers peace of mind.

5. The client is able to take an important action item off their 'to do' list.

Introducing referrals in this manner makes it easy for you and easier for your clients. Additionally, you are facilitating the event and taking the burden off your client which will increase the likelihood of follow through.

The "Meet My Friend" Party Referral

One of the Financial Planner's clients had just opened an art gallery and the current show was very interesting. We asked the owners if they would let us use their space for a SKIRTworking event. We told them we would bring 50 new people to their gallery (free advertising for them) and supply the food, beverages, paper products, and wine glasses as needed. We had the food delivered from Whole Foods ($345) and picked up wine from Costco ($100). Our goal was to bring three guests per member and to divide the cost of the party by the number of the SKIRT™ attendees. The energy at this event was amazing! Several guests asked if they could join our group! Also, a year later, business is still being generated as a result of that event.

Early on in the Mortgage Broker/Financial Planner relationship, they realized many of their clients overlapped so they decided to have a party and bring clients to refer to each other. This is how it worked. They rented out the nicest nail salon in San Francisco and arranged for 30 manicures and pedicures. The Mortgage Broker invited 8 clients that she thought should meet the Financial Planner. She told them she wanted to thank them for their business and they could bring a friend. The Financial Planner invited 7 clients she knew were thinking of buying a home and would need a mortgage so she called and told them her favorite Mortgage Broker and her were throwing a manicure party at a local manicure spa and that she would love to introduce them to the Mortgage Broker and to please bring a friend! They ordered food and champagne and everyone had a great time socializing, getting their nails done and having the opportunity to meet the Mortgage Broker and Financial Planner. Mind you, no business was discussed the whole evening but cards were exchanged! What was an incredibly fun event resulted in much new business from new clients and goodwill from their current clients.

Another take on this was when the Mortgage Broker and Financial Planner rented a private room at an award-winning restaurant in San Francisco. It was a $250 dollar a head dinner and there was room for 10. The Mortgage Broker filled half the table with her clients/guests that she felt should get to know the Financial Planner and the Financial Planner filled half the table with clients/guests that she felt should meet the Mortgage Broker. Note, they also made sure there were name cards on the seats and prearranged who should sit where for maximum effect. Though not the cheapest method to acquire clients (They spent $10,000 at the restaurant in one month!), it is still paying off from word of mouth!

As you go about establishing your SKIRTworking group in accordance with these guidelines, there are a number of things you need to keep in mind:

1. Rome wasn't built in a day!

It's all about relationships! Most often it is not what you know that gets you places in life, but who you know…...Relationships are wonderful, organic things. They are very complex and easy to start, but quite difficult to nurture, rather like plants. When you take an orchid home from the florist, it looks stunning. Buying one is the easy part, but nurturing it, taking the utmost care of it so it continues to bloom season after season, is the difficult task.

For you to trust your fellow SKIRT™ member and for them to trust you enough for them to refer you to one of their contacts, takes time. Unless you have had a long personal or professional relationship with everyone in your group, you are going to tend to refer and receive referrals from those in the group that you know best. Relationships are built on trust and trust needs to be proven and earned. Additionally, just doing a phenomenal job may not always be enough, people are going to want to do business with and spend time with people that display similar character and work ethic. Also, people in the group may already have a strong personal or professional relationship with someone in your area of expertise, so it might take even longer to break the ice.

2. Make a commitment to yourself!

To commit to a cause you need to first make a commitment to make what YOU want a priority. Once the network has established a meeting time and date, make it a non-negotiable item in your calendar. It is easy to fill up our calendar and over book ourselves with activities and functions, but make a mental contract with yourself that this group is going to be a great way for you to build your personal business skills and grow your referral network. In order to successfully speak and market yourself within the group, you need to define what your perfect client is. To be effective in business, it may not be the quantity but the quality of your clients and your return on investment. Make the commitment to yourself to define who this perfect client is and don't forget to ask your group for these types of referrals.

3. Look for pennies in heaven!

How do you find the members you want to have in your group? First, make a list of all of the work and home projects you have done in the last three years. Then, write down the contact information of the professionals that contributed to the project. Rate each person based on their performance. Ask yourself if you would feel comfortable giving their name and number, or better yet, introducing them to one of your friends or family.

Look around your neighborhood and in your community. Perhaps you have had the pleasure of getting to know someone personally, but have never had the opportunity to work with them professionally. If you love their character and personality, you might enjoy having the opportunity to work with them. Make a list of their names, phone numbers and contact information.

The goal is to identify a start list of 10 to 15 people from different professions that are considered stars in their fields. In order for the group to be effective, there can only be one of each profession in the group, to maximize referrals and to not create competition.

4. Choose wisely!

Once a small, diligent, and active group has been established, keep building! Start with 10 to 15 people, others can always be added to the group. What is important is not quantity but quality. Remember the people you refer to your contacts will be a direct reflection of you and your business. If a client or friend is unhappy with the service your fellow SKIRT™ members provide, it could jeopardize your personal and professional relationships with all concerned.

5. When is enough, enough?

The perfect size of the group will be determined by what area of the country you live in and the size of your meeting space. Our experience has been that 20 is a great number. When the group becomes too large, it is difficult to get to know each other in a meaningful way. Having said this, after your group has been successful for several years, and the foundation is built, you may be able to support and handle a group of 20 or more.

6. Consistency

Showing up is half the battle. It is important to make not only the commitment to yourself to attend as many SKIRT™ meetings and events as possible, but you also owe this out of respect to the others in your group. Perhaps someone in the group just met with a new client and has been too busy to call you, but wants to discuss their contact's needs during the hospitality hour. Perhaps a member of the group is having a challenge in their business and knows from past meetings that you have at one time in your personal or professional career encountered a similar challenge and wants your advice. Consistency is opportunity!

7. Aim high!

Set expectations for yourself and other members of the group. The best way to reach a goal is to have a clear understanding of the work that needs to be done to achieve success! The goals and expectations of the group need to be written down. They should also be presented to each new member before they are asked to join the group so they can decide if they are ready to make the level of commitment that SKIRT™ requires. It is very important for individual SKIRT™ members to have a clear understanding of what is expected of them and it is equally important to all of the members of the group as the goal is to hold only one spot in your SKIRT™ Network for each industry or profession. Go to http://www.skirtworking.com to download a sample Commitment

Form™. Remember, making changes and modifications is ok. Depending on your group size, your location and the personal and professional demands of your members, your group may decide to make changes. Do what is necessary for your group to succeed. It is a good idea for the group to review the Group Commitment guidelines on a yearly basis at the Annual Meeting.

8. Get intimate!

As we established early in this chapter, it is all about relationships and relationships take time to nurture and grow. You may want to do business by either receiving or possibly giving referrals to someone in your group, but it is imperative that both of you have a clear understanding of each other's perfect client. Offer to get together one on one for coffee or lunch. We find that for power women, breakfast is a great time of day to meet. In the technology laden world we live in with cell phones, computers and blackberries, perhaps early in the day is a great window of undisturbed time when you can focus on your fellow SKIRT™ member and not be distracted by running your business. The founders of SKIRT™ actually meet once a month outside of the regular SKIRT™ meeting to talk about the group. We discuss what is working, what is not, what changes need to be made and to just have fun. Done right, a breakfast meeting can be the 25th hour in the day!

9. Remember what SKIRT™ means:

Sharing: Share your knowledge and your time. Give first and you will receive- and maybe not from the person you gave to.

Knowledge: Knowledge is power. You can learn more about being a business owner, referrals, and life from the others in your group.

Information: Be a resource for information to the others in your group and to your clients. You will be remembered as the "go to gal".

Resources: Initially the R stood for Referrals. We realized, however, that the resources we provide to our members are so much greater than just the ability to refer business to each other. We provide a website, a forum to share ideas, problems, and solutions, and a place to feel welcome and share in others' successes.

Together: It is not about the individual's success, it is about helping each other create abundance in our lives.

CHAPTER TEN:

Tapping Into Your SKIRT™ Power To Develop Your Average Power

To round off our discussion here, we'd like to introduce you to just one more concept to help drive your networking. The term "average power" (AP) describes something that comes naturally to you, while other people look at you and think you are superhuman. The goal of SKIRT™ is to make networking as natural and fun for women as possible. We want SKIRTworking to become an average power for women because we recognize not only how demanding it is to be in business but also how difficult it is to network using the traditional approach. Let's face it, traditional networking is actually pretty boring. It's also ineffective. SKIRTworking allows you to make the most of your contacts and your innate connector skills. It's also fun and largely informal, which allows you to be your natural, nurturing self. You can also develop a certain confidence being around other women who are talented and dedicated to what they do.

As we outlined, SKIRTworking is about sharing information with women in business. It's about forming long-term partnerships rather than going for a short-term quick-fix. In networking, as in most other instances, the quick-fix approach to getting something is highly overrated and ineffective. It may produce some of the results you want but a week, two weeks, two years down the line, you're going to be in exactly the same place you were in before and you're going to be no happier, no richer, no smarter, and no better overall in terms of how you're living and how well you fit in your own skin.

SKIRTworking, launching your own SKIRT™ Network for businesswomen, brings you the potential to engage with people with similar values and interests in business.

SKIRTworking versus traditional networking allows you to build your own family unit, with every member looking out for the other and building upon natural connections, rather than breeding a short-term, un-motivating environment in which everyone is out to get something for themselves without giving any thought to others.

Women are perfectly capable of fostering strong and mutually beneficial social relationships. Research confirms for us that these relationships improve themselves over time and are far more effective in the long run at bringing us what we want and need.

SKIRT™ Network can bring women the opportunities they need in the most time-efficient and cost-effective manner possible. You don't have to waste your time attending all the other networking groups where you pay a fortune to meet with the same groups of people, the same business professionals stuck in a rut and unsure which way to go. SKIRT™ meetings instead feature women who are longsighted in their goals. Women excel at networking not only because of their nurturing approach but because they do see a bigger picture before them. They see that business contacts can bring client referrals; more than this, they can bring opportunities of all sorts, personal and professional. You can be a client of your fellow SKIRT™ members. They, likewise, can be yours. Overall, you will build and rebuild relationships and you'll find yourself in more control, with more influence over your success than you've ever experienced before.

SKIRTworking will turn networking into just another average power for you and your fellow SKIRTworkers.

Go out and SKIRTwork!

SKIRTworking TERMS:

Commitment Form™: A proprietary tool used by the Membership Chair to secure a full commitment from prospective members. The commitment form should be renewed by active members annually in your SKIRT™ Network.

SKIRT 11 Commandments™: The mandate that SKIRT™ members follow and lead by.

Referral Tracker: A tool for tracking referrals both given and received by SKIRT™ Network members.

Referral Victories: Celebration of the giving and receiving of names of potential clients.

SKIRT™ **Agenda:** An outline or guide to follow when conducting meetings. The agenda is important to keep the meeting on track and concise, and to ensure that all meeting goals are achieved.

SKIRT™: Sharing, Knowledge, Information, and Resources Together.

SKIRT™ **Network:** A group of professionals that come together to develop a referral based business using the philosophies and principles of SKIRT™.

SKIRTworking: A method of networking using SKIRT™.

ABOUT THE AUTHORS

Michelle Alberda has worked in the financial planning industry for over nine years. She founded a solo financial advisory practice in 2007 after earning her CFP© certificant status in 2004. Prior to this, Ms. Alberda worked in South East Asia where she co-founded a consulting firm specializing in government infrastructure projects. She has a degree in Marketing and Asian Studies from Western Michigan University and is a Chartered Life Underwriter.

Michelle Balog is a top real estate agent at one of the highest producing offices in Northern California and ranks in the top 2% of agents in her company nationwide. She has been in the real estate business for seven years and her rapid success is a testament to her networking abilities. Also a talented and accomplished photographer, Michelle ran her own photography business in New York City prior to moving to the Bay Area. She has a degree in film production and photography from the University of Southern California, School of Cinema Television and is a licensed sales agent with the California Department of Real Estate.

With more than 20 years in the financial industry, Stacey Fleece has positioned herself as one of the premier mortgage brokers in the San Francisco Bay Area. She is a Chartered Financial Analyst (CFA) and prior to earning her mortgage license, she worked over 13 years in the hedge fund industry being one of only a handful of women to be General Partner of her own fund. She earned a B.S. in Business with a finance and marketing emphasis from the University of Southern California and a M.A. in Sports Management from the University of San Francisco. She is also a member of the Security Analysts of San Francisco and a licensed sales agent with the California Department of Real Estate.

The careers of Michelle Alberda, Michelle Balog, and Stacey Fleece all began at different times but they came together over seven years ago when Stacey and her husband became clients of Michelle Alberda's financial planning practice. Shortly thereafter, Stacey met Michelle Balog as they were both building their real estate related practices. The three talents met over lunch when Stacey introduced Michelle Alberda to Michelle Balog. By the end of lunch their "dream team" was formed. Not only were they clients of each other, they also regularly referred business to each other.

After realizing that typical marketing and business building techniques were ineffective and too expensive, the three women decided that they wanted to build their businesses entirely by referrals. They knew the power of referrals between the three of them and wanted to capitalize on this power exponentially for themselves while teaching other small businesswomen the power to accelerate their business growth as well. The idea for SKIRTworking was born out of this desire – women helping women build businesses for the collective success of all!

Michelle, Michelle, and Stacey have nearly 40 years of combined experience in the financial services and real estate industries —specifically financial planning, real estate financing, and real estate sales. They founded their women's networking group, SKIRT™, in June of 2005 and the inaugural meeting had seven members in attendance. Since then, the group has grown to over 20 members and a waiting list of interested prospective members has formed. The rewards of membership are numerous and referrals from this group account for upwards of 35% of new business annually for some members. It has proven to be the most cost-effective and efficient way of growing a book of business.

All three women reside in the San Francisco Bay Area and are award-winning, recognized leaders in their chosen fields for both overall production and client acquisition. In addition to their professional successes and SKIRT™, all three women are also active leaders in philanthropic organizations in the Bay Area. Along with many leadership positions and board of director roles, Michelle Alberda is a past President of the Financial Women's Association of San Francisco, Stacey Fleece is a past President of The Junior League of San Francisco and Michelle Balog is a member of the Real Estate Leadership Auxiliary Council for EARN.

ACKNOWLEDGMENTS

A special thanks to the women (and men) in my life who have given the gift of their time, patience and support in helping me pursue my dreams! Thank you to my mother, Carole Alberda, for being a great role model as a rock star mom, a career woman, and a volunteer. My father, James Alberda, told me from a young age that I was as good as, if not better, than the average guy. He also taught me at an early age, how to invest in stock and mutual funds. I took it for granted, Dad, but now I know just how lucky I am to have you around! Thank you to Joanne Healey, Cynthia Kopec, Carrie Riedel, Carrie Rosema, Mary Corroon, Vicky and Doug Struyk, Carly and Juliana Struyk (the solid gold dancers are so inspiring!), my clients, members of the FWA, Whitney Asher, SKIRT™ Network members and my co-authors. I am blessed to be surrounded by such wonderful people who show me unconditional love. – Michelle Alberda

A special thanks to my mother, Sally Balog, for teaching me that all things are possible and that I deserve to succeed. I am the person I am today because of you. A special thanks to my father, Dennis Balog for always being my cheerleader and for teaching me the power of honesty and integrity. Thank you to my brothers, Michael and Christopher Balog, Tera Balog, Dr. Regalena Melrose, Samantha Strickler, Amanda Jones, Dr. Caryn

Wachs, Dr. Sharon Johnson, Tracy Vandenberg, Pat and Wayne Ponik, Sheila Balog and Andrew Lovato. You have all been so supportive and it just wouldn't be fun without you! Very special thanks to my co-authors and dear friends Michelle A. and Stacey. It has been so fun to go on this journey with you and I can't wait to see where it leads us! – Michelle Balog

Heartfelt thanks to my husband, David, and my children, Carson and Piper, for their never-ending support, love and understanding especially during the many long evening and weekend hours spent putting this book together. I also want to thank my mother, Gail, for always being my rock and inspiration and for teaching me that the world is, in fact, my oyster. Thank you to my sisters, Karen and Laurie, and my other "sister", Suzie, for always sharing their love, spirit and laughter. To my dearest friends, Gretchen, Kei and Lezley... thank you for hanging with me on this wild journey of life for the past thirty years. Lastly, very special thanks to Michelle and Michelle – without whom this dream never would have become a reality. – Stacey Fleece

We especially thank the gifted Alicia Dunams for her unwavering support, encouragement and creativity. We couldn't have done it without you! – Michelle, Michelle and Stacey

Want To Start
Your Own SKIRT™ Network?

Want To Learn More About
SKIRTworking?

Go to
www.skirtworking.com

Stop Networking!
Kick up your heels and start
SKIRTworking today!

LaVergne, TN USA
03 October 2010
199442LV00002B/1/P